A BIBLICAL
QUIZ BOOK

QUESTION AND ANSWER

BY

David Olawale Ayinde

CONTENTS

ACKNOWLEDGMENTS

The Bible says we should trust in the Lord always and not to lean on our own understanding; in all our ways we should acknowledge him and He (God) will direct our path (See Proverbs Chapter 3 Verse 5-6).

I want to start by acknowledging God for the inspiration, gift, and talent that he gave me to write this book.

I thank God Almighty for his goodness, grace, love, and mercy. He gives us brand new mercies every day.

There is nothing we cannot accomplish when we put our faith and trust in him.

I would like to acknowledge: Wintershall Passion Plays, Time Life, Fulaba, and Cecil Blount Demille Foundation whose resources have contributed generously to the publication of this book.

I would also like to thank the Pastors, who have been a positive influence in my life when preaching the Gospel, and my History Teachers who made the subject very interesting for me to study in school. This book would not have been possible without their influence.

THANKS

I would like to thank my wife, Patricia Ngozi Uloma Ayinde, for doing an amazing job checking the accuracy of the book. She has been a constant encouragement and inspiration to me in getting this book written and published.

I thank my parents, grandparents, in-laws, brother, cousins, uncles, and aunts.

I also like to thank all those people that I have worked with over the years that have been a positive influence to help me focus to get this book written.

ABOUT THE AUTHOR

David Olawale Ayinde was born in Stepney Mile End, East London. He is married to his lovely wife Patricia Ngozi Ayinde.

At the age of 10 his parents took him and his brother to Nigeria to gain a knowledge and appreciation of where his parents originated from. He completed his primary and secondary education in Nigeria before returning to the UK where he completed his further education.

In school, he excelled in English Literature, History, and Religious Biblical Knowledge.

He studied Social Science at University of Westminster and graduated with a BA (Hons) Degree in Social Science. He has worked for various departments in the UK Civil Service, and currently works in the UK Security Sector.

He is also a trained professional actor. David graduated from Rose Bruford Theatre College, obtaining a Certificate in Theatre & Arts (Acting) and at the London Actors Workshop.

He was involved in the 2017 Easter Production Re-enactment of the Passion of Christ in Trafalgar Square.

You can also find more about the author by going to: https://www.imdb.com/name/nm6454657/

AN INSPIRING WORD

FROM THE AUTHOR

I have been looking forward to writing my first book and what better way to start by writing an academic Biblical Quiz Book.

It is a suitable resource for anyone; whatever their level of Biblical Knowledge; basic, intermediate, or advanced you will find the book refreshing, educational, fun, and resourceful. It covers multiple-choice questions on both the Old and New Testament parts of the Bible.

I hope that you will find this book academically challenging and spiritually beneficial.

PREFACE

Philosopher Immanuel Kant once quoted, "The existence of the Bible as a book for the people is the greatest benefit which the human race has ever experienced."

I have always had a genuine interest in reading fascinating biblical stories and bringing them to light.

This book has helped to fulfil that goal.

It is a useful learning resource that can be used for:

a) Primary, Secondary, and advanced level;

b) Bible School Teachers;

c) Christian Theologians; and

d) Individuals that want to gain a knowledge and understanding of the Bible.

This multiple-choice Bible test book came about through extensive Jewish, Christian, and Religious Historic Research.

The book is a combination of True or False and multiple-choice questions.

It is a must read that will increase your knowledge and interest in the Bible.

SECTION ONE

QUESTIONS

1) Name the first book of the Bible.

2) How many books does the Bible consist of?

3) Where can the book of Malachi be found in the Bible?

4) Who wrote Psalm 23 in the Bible?

5) Name the disciples that accompanied Jesus Christ to the Mountain of Transfiguration.

6) How many children did Jacob's first wife bare?

7) Who gave birth to Dan and Naphtali?

8) Mention the name of Gad and Asher's Mother.

9) Who did Rachel, Jacob's second wife, give birth to?

10) How many times did God call Samuel?

11) Name three known Nazarites in the Bible.

12) Why was God more pleased with Abel's Sacrifice Offering than his brother Cain?

13) Mention the names of King David's sisters in the Bible.

14) Who were King David's parents?

15) What was Ruth's original nationality?

16) Who was Absalom?

17) Why was King Saul jealous of David?

18) Explain briefly how Joab was appointed Commander-In-Chief of the army during David's reign as King Israel?

19) Where can the book of Exodus be found in the Bible?

20) Name five of King David's known wives mentioned in the Bible.

21) What are the names of Noah's children?

22) How long did the flood last in the Book of Genesis?

23) Who was Esau?

24) What led to the feud between Esau and Jacob?

25) Who were the Jebusites in the Old Testament of the Bible?

26) Define the meaning of the name Moses.

27) Why did Jacob like Joseph more than his other sons?

28) Who led the Israelites into the Promise Land in the Bible?

29) Why did Moses not enter the Promise Land?

30) Where did Aaron die and at what age?

31) Who were Joseph's two sons in the Bible?

32) Who was Asenath?

33) Who was Joseph sold to for twenty pieces of silver?

34) Mention the names of the Patriarchs according to Hebrew Ancestry.

35) Who are the Matriarchs according to Hebrew Ancestry?

36) Name the five books of Moses in the Old Testament of the Bible.

37) Briefly describe who Samson was in the Bible.

38) What was the role of the Judges in the Bible before the Monarchy of the Unified Israel?

39) What tribe of Israel was King Saul from?

40) Who was Lot and what happened to his wife?

41) In the Bible, where do the Moabites and Ammonites originate from?

42) Name Prophet Samuel's Parents in the Bible.

43) Why was King Saul rejected as King of the Unified Monarchy of Israel?

44) Briefly discuss why God punished Eli and his family.

45) Why did Phinehas' wife name her child Ichabod?

46) Why was Miriam struck with Leprosy?

47) Who was Zipporah in the Bible?

48) What does Gershom mean in the Bible?

49) What are the four Gospels in the New Testament of the Bible?

50) Why were Adam and Eve driven out of the Garden of Eden?

51) Who was Abraham's father in the Bible?

52) In the Bible, what did God say he would make Abraham?

53) According to the Bible, what leader led the ancient Israelites into the Promise Land?

54) Who was Caleb in the Bible?

55) What other name was Joshua, the son of Nun, called in the Bible?

56) Why were Joshua and Caleb of a different spirit?

57) Explain who Rehab was in the Bible.

58) Who was Eli in the Bible?

59) What were names of Eli's sons?

60) Who were Samuel's sons in the Bible?

61) Why did the ancient Israelites demand a king when Samuel grew old?

62) Define the meaning of the name Samuel in the Bible.

63) Explain who the Amalekites were in the Bible?

64) Who was Jethro in the Bible?

65) Name nine women in the Bible (Old Testament) that played a significant role.

66) Mention three of David's brothers in the Bible.

67) Who was Jonathan in the Bible?

68) Who was the first king of the Unified Monarchy of Israel?

69) Who was Abner in the Bible?

70) Who was Ishbosheth in the Bible?

71) In the Bible, what did David do in Cave Adullam?

72) Who was Ahithophel in the Bible?

73) Who was Hushai in the Bible?

74) Who was King David's fourth child?

75) Why did King Saul later become jealous of David?

76) Briefly explain why you think King David temporarily had Joab removed as Commander-in-chief of the Unified army of ancient Israel.

77) How long did King David rule over all of the Unified Monarchy of Israel?

78) Who was Sheba, son of Bicri, and how was his revolt against King David repelled?

79) Briefly describe how David slew Goliath.

80) Who was Ahimelech and how did he help David in the Bible?

81) Why was God very angry with King Solomon?

82) Where did David eventually flee to prevent King Saul from killing him?

83) What did the Queen of Sheba do when she heard of King Solomon's fame and wisdom?

84) In the Bible, explain why the Unified Kingdom of Israel split after the reign of King Solomon?

85) Name in the Bible which one of King David's courageous men went to take the stronghold city of The Jebusites?

86) Which one of King David's mighty men went into a pit on a snowy day and killed a lion?

87) Who was Jabez in the Bible?

88) Who was Lot in the Bible?

89) What happened to Lot's wife in the Bible?

90) Who is the father of Moab and Ammon?

91) How did Asahel die?

92) What did Solomon ask from God?

93) How long were the ancient Israelites in ancient Egypt for?

94) Name two manipulative female characters in the Bible.

95) Who was Jehoshaphat in the Bible?

96) Explain who Ahab was in the Bible.

97) Briefly describe who Elijah was in the Bible

98) Name the disciple that betrayed Jesus Christ in the Bible.

99) In the Bible, who murdered Naboth for his Vineyard?

100) Who was Jezebel in the Bible?

101) Briefly explain what Jehu's mission was in the Bible.

102) Mention who Mordecai was in the Bible.

103) Explain who the antagonist was in the book of Esther.

104) What other name was Solomon known by in the Bible?

105) List the twelve Minor Prophets in the Old Testament of the Bible.

106) Who was Rehoboam in the Bible?

107) Who was Jeroboam in the Bible?

108) Briefly describe who Naaman was in the Bible.

109) Who was King Abijah in the Bible?

110) List the Major Prophets in the Old Testament.

111) What happened at Zarephath when Prophet Elijah went there?

112) Mention two characters in the Bible that were 'gifted by God' to interpret dreams.

113) Describe the Book of Lamentations in the Bible.

114) Who was Jonah? And why was he swallowed up by a whale?

115) Explain briefly who the people of ancient Nineveh were in the Bible.

116) Who were Daniel's friends in the Book of Daniel?

117) Define the meaning of the name Daniel in the Bible.

118) Who was Nebuchadnezzar II in the Bible?

119) Define briefly the Neo-Assyrian Empire.

120) What does MENE, MENE, TEKEL, PARSIN mean in the Bible?

121) Who were Elizabeth and Zachariah in the Bible?

122) Describe who John the Baptist was in the Bible.

123) Who was the last King of ancient Judah before its fall to King Nebuchadnezzar II?

124) Describe who Elisha's servant was in the Bible.

125) Who showed hospitality to Prophet Elisha in the Bible?

126) What other name was Solomon's Temple known as?

127) Who was Naaman in the Bible?

128) According to the Bible, what did John the Baptist eat?

129) In the Bible, how long did Jonah spend in the belly of the whale?

130) Mentioned in the Bible, who was described as the 'Forerunner' of Jesus Christ?

SECTION TWO

QUESTIONS

131) Who wrote the Gospel of Matthew in the New Testament of the Bible?

132) Mention who the Law Giver in the Old Testament of the Bible was.

133) Who was Matthew's Gospel in the New Testament originally written for?

134) Mention who tempted Jesus Christ in the Bible after his baptism by John the Baptist.

135) Name the Four Fisherman Jesus called to become Disciples.

136) How many Books are in the New Testament of the Bible?

137) Who wrote the Gospel of Luke in the New Testament of the Bible?

138) How many Books did Apostle Paul write in the New Testament of the Bible?

139) Who persecuted the Early Church in the Book of Acts of Apostles before their conversion?

140) Who denied knowing Jesus Christ in the Bible when the rooster crowed three times?

141) Mention who wrote the Books of I Peter and II Peter in the Bible?

142) Discuss briefly which Christian follower was martyred first in the Book of Acts.

143) Which disciple tried to walk on water when coming to meet Jesus Christ in the Bible?

144) Who was the Apostle Andrew in the Bible?

145) What happened to Ananias and Sapphira?

146) Who was the Angel Gabriel in the Bible?

147) Mention what happened on the Day of Pentecost in the Book of Acts.

148) Describe the term 'Gentile(s)' in the Bible.

149) Narrate the story of the ancient Ethiopian Eunuch in the Bible.

150) Name the gifts that the Wise Men presented to Baby Jesus Christ.

151) How old was Jesus Christ when he began his Ministry?

152) What did Herod do when he realised that he had been deceived by the Wise Men?

153) Where did the Angel instruct Joseph to take Baby Jesus Christ and Mary to escape Herod's wrath?

154) What was Jesus Christ's first miracle recorded in the Bible?

155) In the Bible, what does John Chapter 3 Verse 16 say?

156) What does John Chapter 1 Verses 1 say in the Bible?

157) In the Bible, who was sent to restore Saul's sight? (Who later became Paul)

158) Who replaced Judas Iscariot in joining the disciples as stated in the Bible?

159) Briefly describe how the Gospel of John portrays Jesus Christ in the New Testament of the Bible. How does John's Gospel differ from Matthew and Luke's Gospel?

160) In the Bible, who did Jesus Christ cite as an example to say was the greatest in the kingdom of heaven?

161) In Matthew Chapter 17 Verse 10-13 of the New Testament, mention who was being referred to as "Elijah must come first".

162) Quote John Chapter 14 Verse 1 in the Bible.

163) In the Bible, explain what you think can be learnt from the story of how the woman with the issue of blood was healed.

164) What do you understand by the term 'Canonical Gospels' in the Bible?

165) Briefly explain why you think John's Gospel is not part of the Canonical or Synoptic Gospels.

166) Describe the significance of the "Parable of the Lost Sheep".

167) In the Bible, what were the Scribes and Chief Priests' reaction to Jesus Christ when he taught in the temple?

168) Describe briefly, from the Bible, what Apostles Peter and John did at the Temple of the Beautiful Gate.

169) Explain briefly what can be learnt about the "Parable of The Persistent Widow"?

170) What did Judas Iscariot do in the Garden of Gethsemane?

171) According to the Bible, what did the blind beggar Bartimaeus shout out when he heard that Jesus Christ was nearby?

172) In the Bible, what did Jesus Christ say were the two most important commandments?

173) Explain briefly why Seven Deacons were chosen by the Apostles in the Book of Acts.

174) Name the Seven Deacons chosen in the Book of Acts of Apostles.

175) In the Bible, name the six pieces of the armour of God.

176) According to the Bible, where was the Apostle Timothy born?

177) Briefly mention what the Apostle Paul's charge to his protégé Timothy was in the Bible.

178) Who was Lydia in the Bible?

179) What can be learnt about 'The Book of Hebrews'?

180) Define the term 'The Fruit of The Holy Spirit'

SECTION THREE

ANSWER TRUE OR FALSE

181) In the Bible, the name "Immanuel" or "Emmanuel" means "God is with us".

True or False? (Matthew Chapter 1 Verse 23)

182) Abel was the first character in The Old Testament of the Bible murdered by his brother Cain.

True or False? (Genesis Chapter 4 Verse 8)

183) King Solomon obeyed God throughout his reign.

True or False. (I Kings Chapter 11 Verse 1-13)

184) In the Bible, Joab was first Commander-in-Chief of Judah army before being promoted to Commander-in-Chief of the Unified Kingdom of Israel army.

True or False? (I Samuel Chapter 2 Verse 13-30)

185) The ancient Israelites in the Old Testament were punished when they did evil in the sight of God and served false gods.

True or False? (Judges Chapter 2 Verse 11-17)

186) King Nebuchadnezzar in the Bible was a friendly ally to the ancient Israelites.

True or False? (II King Chapter 24 Verse 10-16; Daniel Chapter 1 Verse 1)

187) In the Bible, John the Baptist was described as "The Forerunner" of Jesus Christ.

True or False? (Isaiah Chapter 40 Verse 3; Matthew Chapter 3 Verse 1-12)

188) Psalms 119 is the shortest chapter in the Bible.

True or False? (Psalms Chapter 119 Verse 1-176)

189) The Apostle Paul in the Bible was one of the original twelve apostles of Jesus Christ.

True or False? (Matthew Chapter 10 Verse 1-4)

190) In the Bible, Jesus Christ is described as coming from the lineage of King David.

True or False? (Matthew Chapter 1 Verse 1-17)

191) Jesus Christ never healed on the Sabbath day.

True or False? (Luke Chapter 6 Verse 6-11)

192) The Gospel of John Chapter 10 describes that thief (Satan) comes to "steal", "kill", and "destroy".

True or False? (John Chapter 10 Verse 10)

193) The Book of Acts of Apostles in the Bible is about the

death of the Apostles.

Truth or False? (Acts of Apostles Chapter 1-Acts of Apostles Chapter 28)

194) Peter denied Jesus Christ before the rooster crowed three times.

True or False?

195) King David's personal problems began when he killed Uriah and took his wife.

True or False? (II Samuel Chapter 12 Verse 10-12)

196) After leading the Royal Israelite Forces of King David to victory at the Battle of the Wood of Ephraim against the Rebel Forces of the exiled Israelite Prince Absalom, Joab was removed as Commander-in-Chief of the ancient Unified Kingdom of Israel army.

True or False? (II Samuel Chapter 19 Verse 1-13)

197) In the Bible, Solomon asked God for wisdom to rule over the Unified Kingdom of Israel.

True or False? (I Kings Chapter 3 Verse 7-15)

198) One of the miracles in the Bible that Jesus Christ performed was the feeding of Five Thousand People.

True or False?

199) Mark, Andrew, and Jude were the disciples taken by Jesus Christ to the Mountain of Transfiguration.

True or False? (Matthew Chapter 17 Verse 1-9)

200) In the Book of Acts of Apostles in the Bible, the early Believers who believed in the Gospel of Jesus Christ were all united and were of one heart and one soul.

True or False? (Acts of Apostles Chapter 4 Verse 32-37)

201) The miracle of Jesus Christ healing the Roman's Centurion servant is recorded in all four Gospels in The New Testament of the Bible.

True or False.

SECTION FOUR

ANSWER A, B, C, D, OR E

202) What Biblical Character uttered the following words?: *"I am not worthy that you should come under my roof. But just only speak a word, and my servant will be healed. For I am a under authority; having soldiers under me. And I say to this one, go and he goes; and to another come, and he comes, and to my servant do this, and he does it."*

(Matthew Chapter 8 Verse 5-13; Luke Chapter 7 Verse 1-10)

A) Apostle Peter

B) King Solomon

C) Prophet Elijah

D) The Roman Centurion

E) Absalom

203) What Biblical Character said the following?: *"An evil and adulterous generation seeks after a sign, and no sign will be given except the sign of the Prophet Jonah. For as Jonah was three days and three nights in the belly of the great whale, so will The Son of Man be three days and three nights in the heart of the earth. The people of Nineveh will rise up in the judgement with this generation and condemn it, because they repented at the preaching of Jonah; and indeed, a greater than Jonah is here. The queen of the South will rise up in the judgement with this generation and condemn it, for she came from the ends of the earth to hear the wisdom of Solomon; and indeed, a greater than Solomon is here."*

(Matthew Chapter 12 Verse 39-42)

A) Jesus Christ

B) King David

C) Apostle Peter

D) Prophet Samuel

E) None of the above

204) Who uttered these words in the Bible?: *"Brood of Vipers! Who warned you to flee of the wrath to come? Therefore bear fruits worthy of repentance, and do not think to say to yourselves, we have Abraham as our father. For I say to you that God is able to raise up children to Abraham from these stones."*

(Matthew Chapter 3 Verse 7-9)

A) Prophet Jeremiah

B) King Solomon

C) Moses

D) Prophet Elisha

E) John the Baptist

205) Name the Biblical Character who said the following words: *"We saved your life today and the lives of your sons, your daughters, your wives, and concubines. Yet you act like this, making us feel ashamed of ourselves. You seem to love those who hate you and hate those who love you. You have made it clear today that your commanders and troops mean nothing to you. It seems that if Absalom had lived and all of us had died you would be pleased. Now go out there and congratulate your troops, for I swear by the Lord that if you don't go out, not a single one of them will remain here tonight. Then you will be worse off than ever before."*

(II Samuel Chapter 19 Verse 5-7)

A) Jehu

B) Joshua

C) Samson

D) Joab

E) Abner

206) What Biblical Character wrote the following?: *"The beauty of Israel is slain on high places! How the mighty have fallen! Tell it not in Gath. Proclaim it not in the streets of Ashkelon. Lest the daughters of the Philistines rejoice. Lest the daughters of the uncircumcised triumph. O mountains of Gilboa. Let there be no dew nor rain upon you. Nor fields of offerings for the shield of the mighty is cast away there! The shield of Saul not anointed with oil. From the blood of the slain. From the fat of the mighty. The bow of Jonathan did not turn back. And the sword of Saul did not return empty. Saul and Jonathan were beloved and pleasant in their lives. And in their death they were not divided. They were swifter than eagles. They were stronger than lions. O daughters of Israel, weep over Saul who clothed you in scarlet with luxury. Who put ornaments of gold on your apparel. How the mighty have fallen in the midst of the battle! Jonathan was slain in your high places. I am distressed for you my brother Jonathan. You were very pleasant to me. Your love to me was wonderful. Surpassing the love of women. How the mighty have fallen, and the weapons of war perished!"*

(II Samuel Chapter 1 Verse 19-27)

A) King David

B) Prophet Jeremiah

C) Abigail

D) Joab

E) None of the above

207) Name the Biblical Character who uttered the following words: *"If you hadn't ploughed with my heifer, you wouldn't have solved my riddle."*

(Judges Chapter 14 Verse 18)

A) Gideon

B) Ashael

C) Nathan

D) Jonathan

E) Samson

208) Which Biblical Character uttered the following words: *"Whoever attacks the Jebusites first shall be chief and captain of the army."*

(I Chronicles Chapter 11 Verse 6)

A) King Saul

B) Moses

C) King David

D) King Josiah

E) None of the above

209) Where in the Bible can the following words be found?: *"Let him kiss me with the kisses of his mouth. For your love is better than wine."*

(Song of Solomon Chapter 1 Verse 1)

A) The Book of Genesis

B) The Songs of Solomon

C) The Book of Proverbs

D) The Book of Job

E) The Gospel of John

210) Which of the following Prophets in the Old Testament of the Bible foretold the following words?: *"For a child is born*

to us, a son is given to us. The government will rest on his shoulders, and He will be called Wonderful Counsellor, Mighty God, Everlasting Father, and Prince of Peace. His government and its peace will never end."

(Isaiah Chapter 9 Verse 6-7)

A) Prophet Elijah

B) Prophet Nathan

C) Prophet Isaiah

D) Prophet Samuel

E) Prophet Jonah

211) In the Bible, mention who Jesus Christ was referring to when he said the following statement: *"Can the friends of the Bridegroom fast while the Bridegroom is with them? As long as they have the Bridegroom with them, they cannot fast. But the days will come when the Bridegroom will be taken away from them, and then they will fast."*

(Matthew Chapter 9 Verse 15)

A) The Disciples who later became known as Apostles

B) The Gentiles

C) The Pharisees

D) The Persians

E) The Philistines

212) Which of the following apostles wrote the following statement in the Bible?: *"For I am not ashamed of the Gospel (Good News) about Christ. It is the power of God at work, saving everyone who believes – the Jew first and then to the Gentile."*

(Romans Chapter 1 Verse 16)
A) The Apostle Peter

B) The Apostle James

C) The Apostle Paul (formerly known as Saul)

D) The Apostle Thaddaeus

E) None of the above

213) In the Bible, who was Jesus Christ referring to when he said the following?: *"Blessed are you Simon Barjona, because flesh and blood did not reveal this to you, but my Father (God) who is in heaven."*

(Matthew Chapter 16 Verse 17)

A) Apostle Simon the Cananite

B) Stephen

C) Simon the Sorcerer

D) King David

E) Apostle Peter (also known as Simon Peter)

214) Mention who Jesus Christ was referring to when he said the following: *"Haven't you read in the Scriptures what David did when he and his companions were hungry? He went into the House of God, and he and his companions broke the law by eating the sacred loaves of bread that only the priests were allowed to eat, and haven't you read in the Law of Moses that the priests on duty in the Temple may work on the Sabbath? I tell you there is one here who is even greater than the Temple! But you would not have condemned my innocent disciples if you knew the meaning of this Scripture. I want you to show mercy, not offer sacrifices. For the Son of Man is Lord even over the Sabbath!"*

(Matthew Chapter 12 Verse 3-8; Luke Chapter 6 Verse 3-5)

A) The Romans

B) The Ammonites

C) The Jebusites

D) The Pharisees

E) The Perizzites

215) What ancient Israel Army Commander-in-Chief in the Bible uttered the following words?: *"If the Arameans (The Syrians of Zobah and Rehob) are too strong for me, then come over and help me; and if the Ammonites are too strong for you, I will come and help you. Be courageous! Let us fight bravely for our people and the cities of our God. May the Lord's will be done."*

(II Samuel Chapter 10 Verse 12; I Chronicles Chapter 19 Verse 13)

A) Jehu

B) Joshua

C) Joab

D) Amasa

E) Abner

216) Mention which Biblical Character said the following: *"You come to me with a sword, with a spear, and with a javelin; but I come to you in the name of the Lord of hosts, the God of the armies of Israel, whom you have defied. This day the Lord will deliver you into my hand, and I will strike you and take your head from you, and this day I will give the carcasses of the camp of the Philistines to the birds of the air and the wild beasts of the earth, that all the earth may know that there is a God in Israel. Then all the assembly shall know that the Lord does not save with sword and spear; for the battle in the Lord's, and he will deliver you into our hands (Israel)."*

(I Samuel Chapter 17 Verse 45-47)

A) Samson

B) Jehu

C) Abner

D) Esau

E) David

217) Job was from the land of:

(See Job Chapter 1 Verse 1; Genesis Chapter 10 Verse 22-23)

A) Judah

B) Zoo

C) Gaza

D) UZ

E) Dan

218) Job's children were killed instantly by":

(See Job Chapter 1 Verse 19)

A) Famine

B) Arson

C) Great wind

D) Earthquake

E) Flood

219) The boils that were afflicted on Job came from:

(See Job Chapter 2 Verse 7)

A) His wife

B) God

C) His children

D) His friends

E) Satan

220) In the Book of Romans, who was Apostle Paul addressing?

(See Romans Chapter 1 Verse 7)

A) The descendants of King David

B) Roman Citizens

C) The Jews

D) Christians in Rome

E) The Gentiles

221) The Gospel of John in the Bible commences with:

(See John Chapter 1 Verse 1-15)

A) A paean to the word of God

B) A genealogy of Jesus Christ

C) A foretelling of Prophet Isaiah about Jesus Christ the Messiah

D) The Resurrection of Jesus Christ

E) Restoring of the Kingdom of King David

222) In the Book of Genesis, on the first day God said:

(See Genesis Chapter 1 Verse 3-5)

A) I will bless mankind

B) I found David, the son of Jesse, a man after my own heart, who will do all my will

C) Let there be light

D) Let there be a firmament

E) Let the earth bring forth grass

223) Zacchaeus the tax collector, who sought to see Jesus Christ, climbed up into a sycamore tree because he was:

(See Luke Chapter 19 Verse 2-4)

A) A lunatic

B) Short in stature

C) Shy

D) A talkative

E) Afraid

224) The Seven Churches to where John was to send his account of the revelation included:

(See Revelation Chapter 1 Verse 11)

A) Benfica

B) Greece

C) Damascus

D) Philadelphia

E) Jerusalem

225) In the Book of Revelations, with the church in Philadelphia the Spirit of God was evidently:

(See Revelation Chapter 3 Verse 7-13; Revelation Chapter 2 Verse 29)

A) Well Pleased

B) Moderately Pleased

C) Not pleased

D) Angry

E) Unhappy

226) The Book of Revelations reveals the Spirit of God was displeased with the Laodicean Church because it was:

(See Revelations Chapter 3 Verse 14-16)

A) Wicked

B) Hypocritical

C) Lukewarm

D) Extravagant

E) Faithful

227) The Bible says in the Book of Proverbs that it is better to be in the corner of the housetop than with a:

(See Proverbs Chapter 25 Verse 24)

A) Insane Woman

B) Attractive Woman

C) Spy

D) Pauper

E) Contentious Wife/Woman

228) Hope deferred makes the:

(See Proverbs Chapter 13 Verse 12)

A) Heart sick

B) Soul resourceful

C) Head Swell

D) Mind go crazy

E) Spirit tough

229) A soft answer turns away:

(See Proverbs Chapter 15 Verse 1)

A) Pride

B) Wrath

C) Joy

D) Opportunities

E) Progress

230) The Book of Genesis states that God created man from:
(See Genesis Chapter 2 Verse 7)

A) Science

B) Oxygen

C) Dust

D) Mud

E) Bionics

231) Jesus Christ gave his twelve disciples the power to:

(See Matthew Chapter 10 Verse 1)

A) Cast out unclean spirits

B) Be competitive

C) Marry more than one wife

D) Turn water into wine

E) Tell Parables

232) The Acts of the Apostles was written by:

A) Peter

B) Moses

C) Joab

D) Paul

E) Luke

233) King David in the Book of Psalms praises God Almighty for having made human beings: (See Psalm Chapter 8 Verse 5)

A) Equal to Angels

B) A little lower than Angels

C) Far lower than Angels

D) To worship Angels

E) To make sacrifices to Angels

234) The Apostle Paul wrote that, five times he had received: (See II Corinthians Chapter 11 Verse 24)

A) Bribes to keep quiet

B) Forty stripes minus one

C) Three stripes

D) Ten stripes

E) Thirty stripes plus one

235) Jesus Christ's exclamation, "Verily I say unto you, I have not found so great faith, no, not in Israel" was elicited by the words of:

(See Matthew Chapter 8 Verse 5-10)

A) Cornelius (A Centurion of the Italian Regiment)

B) Apostle Paul

C) The woman suffering from a haemorrhage of blood (for twelve years)

D) The Centurion

E) Peter's mother-in-law

236) Jesus Christ healed the paralytic because He (Jesus Christ):

(See Matthew Chapter 9 Verse 1-8)

A) Wanted the Scribes to know that He (Jesus Christ) had the power to forgive sins

B) Did not want to show favouritism

C) He only wanted to heal the Gentiles because they had great faith

D) He (the person) would become a disciple

E) None of the above

237) Zephaniah was a descendant of:

(See Zephaniah Chapter 1 Verse 1)

A) Absalom

B) Prophet Isaiah

C) Prophet Nathan

D) Job

E) Hezekiah

238) David knew he could subdue Goliath because:

(See I Samuel Chapter 17 Verse 32-37)

A) He was the youngest of his brothers

B) He put his trust in God and had killed a Lion and a Bear when they came after his father's sheep

C) He (David) was untouchable

D) He knew he could rely on his best friend Jonathan to help

E) He (David) had experience of mountain climbing

239) David's armoury when he was about to take on Goliath consisted of a sling and smooth stones to the number of:

(See I Samuel Chapter 17 Verse 40)

A) Five

B) Three

C) Two

D) One

E) Four

240) David's cry, "O my son Absalom," was one of:

(See II Samuel Chapter 18 Verse 33)

A) Promotion

B) Celebration

C) Grief

D) Recognition

E) Scorn

241) John the Baptist's food was:

(See Matthew Chapter 3 Verse 4)

A) Salmon and leaves

B) Honey and Pancakes

C) Turnip

D) Manna

E) Locust and wild honey

242) The Lord God expressed his attitude towards divorce as one of:

(See Malachi Chapter 2 Verse 16)

A) Tolerance

B) Hate

C) Joy

D) Acceptance

E) Compromise

243) Jesus Christ was led up into the wilderness by:

(See Matthew Chapter 4 Verse 1)

A) Angels

B) His disciples

C) The Spirit of God

D) The Psalm 23

E) Prophet Elijah

244) When the devil urged Jesus Christ to prove himself as the Son of God by throwing himself down from the pinnacle of the temple, Jesus responded that:

(See Matthew Chapter 4 Verse 5-7)

A) He (Jesus) would rather turn water into wine

B) Having disarmed principalities and powers, He (Jesus) made a public spectacle of them, triumphing over them in it

C) It is written, "Thou shall not tempt the Lord thy God"

D) Get behind me Satan!

E) It is written, "Man shall not live by bread alone"

245) Queen Vashti was removed from her position for her disobedience because the king feared that:

(See Esther Chapter 1 Verse 10-19)

A) All wives in the province would follow her example

B) All wives will ridicule their husbands

C) She (Vashti) could develop some dangerous ideas

D) Husbands will be afraid of their wives

E) None of the above

246) The Apostle Paul as a speaker evidently considered himself as:
(See II Corinthians Chapter 11 Verse 6)
A) An effective Orator

B) A showman

C) A rival to Apostle Peter

D) Untrained in speech

E) Shy

247) Apostles Peter and John were arrested because the Priests, the Sadducees, and the Captain of temple were grieved by their (Peter and John):

(See Acts Chapter 4 Verse 1-3)

A) Preaching in Solomon's Porch (Portico)

B) Healing without a licence

C) Speaking in foreign tongues

D) Inciting a riot

E) Preaching the Gospel and the Resurrection of Jesus Christ

248) The marriage present King Saul asked of David was:
(See I Samuel Chapter 18 Verse 25)

A) The head of Goliath

B) A hundred foreskins of the Ammonites

C) A hundred foreskins of the Philistines

D) The Gates of Gaza

249) Who was David's best friend in the Bible?

(See II Samuel Chapter 1 Verse 17-27)

A) Jonathan

B) Abner

C) Amasa

D) Ishbosheth

E) Mephibosheth

250) David would have nearly been killed by Saul if it was not because of:

(See I Samuel Chapter 19 Verse 1-17)

A) Samuel

B) Abner

C) Jonathan and Michal (King Saul's son and daughter)

D) Eliab

E) Abishai

251) David resisted the urge to kill King Saul at the Wilderness of En Gedi because:

(See I Samuel Chapter 24 Verse 1-22)

A) He (David) recognised that King Saul was God's anointed.

B) He (David) had sympathy for King Saul

C) He (David) was having a bad day

D) He (David) did not want to jeopardise his friendship with Jonathan

E) He (David) was madly in love with Michal

252) King Solomon had:

(See I Kings Chapter 10 Verse 26)

A) 10,000 Chariots

B) 1,400 Chariots

C) 14,000 Chariots

D) 15,000 Chariots

E) 14,500 Chariots

253) King Solomon wrote:

(See I Kings Chapter 4 Verse 32)

A) 100 proverbs and 100 psalms

B) 200 psalms and 150 proverbs

C) 380 proverbs and 29 songs

D) 3,000 songs and 1,005 proverbs

E) 3,000 Proverbs and 1,005 songs

254) God allowed Rehoboam to only rule over a small portion of ancient Israel because:

(See I Kings Chapter 12 Verse 17-20, I Kings Chapter 11 Verse 4-13)

A) God did not think that Rehoboam was up to the task of ruling the whole of the Unified Kingdom of Israel

B) Solomon treacherously murdered his brother Adonijah (who was the rightful heir) to succeed their father David

C) Of Solomon's apostasy

D) Absalom's treason

E) Rehoboam's harshness

255) Solomon had:

(See I Kings Chapter 11 Verse 3)

A) 700 wives and 300 concubines

B) 7,000 concubines and 30 wives

C) 1 wife

D) No wives

E) 300 wives

256) Jesus Christ cried out: "Father, forgive them; for they know not what they do," when He was:

(See Luke Chapter 23 Verse 33-34)

A) Condemned by Pontius Pilate

B) Baptised by John the Baptist

C) Accused of socialising with Tax Collectors and Sinners

D) Scoffed and mocked by bystanders

E) Crucified

257) "My God, my God, why have thou forsaken me?" cried"
(See Matthew Chapter 27 Verse 46)

A) Jesus Christ to God

B) God to King Solomon

C) Peter before the rooster crowed thrice

D) When Daniel was cast into the lion's den

E) When Lot's wife turned into a pillar of salt

258) In the Old Testament of the Bible, Deborah, the wife of Lapidoth, was a:

(See Judges Chapter 4 Verse 4-5)

A) Stay-at-home mother

B) Opportunist

C) Tax Collector

D) Prophetess & Judge

E) Queen

259) Which of the following in the Bible was a Nazarite?:
(See Judges Chapter 13 Verse 7)

A) Absalom

B) Benaiah

C) Esau

D) Samson

E) Ruth

260) "For thou shalt heap coals of fire upon his head" by giving a thirsty enemy:
(See Proverbs 25 Verse 21-22)

A) Water to drink

B) Poison to drink

C) Acid to drink

D) Nothing to drink

E) Oil to drink

261) A good man leaves an inheritance to:
(See Proverbs Chapter 13 Verse 22)

A) Nobody

B) A fool

C) His children's children

D) A Stranger

E) The Church

262) As a dog returns to its vomit, so does:

(See Proverbs Chapter 26 Verse 11)

A) An unbeliever return to their unbelief

B) A sluggard return to their couch

C) A fool return to their folly

D A person return to their pride

E) It needs to learn new tricks

263) "I am the Alpha and Omega," said:

(See Revelations Chapter 1 Verse 8)

A) Jesus Christ

B) Angel Gabriel

C) John the Baptist

D) Martha

E) Esther

264) He who finds a wife finds:

(See Proverbs Chapter 18 Verse 22)

A) Trouble

B) Controversy

C) A good thing

D) Stress

E) Competition

265) Jezebel was:

(See I Kings Chapter 16 Verse 29-31)

A) The sister to Delilah

B) Samson's wife

C) Absalom's wife

D) Rehoboam's wife

E) Ahab's wife

266) Which one of the following was a close relative to King David?:

(See I Chronicles Chapter 2 Verse 13-17)

A) Abel

B) Joab

C) Job

D) Joseph

E) Jehu

267) Moses was:

(See Numbers Chapter 20 Verse 1-12)

A) Permitted by God to lead the ancient Israelites into the Promise Land

B) Not permitted by God to lead the ancient Israelites into the Promise Land

C) Permitted by God to lead them in war against their enemies

D) Permitted to lead them in idol worshipping

E) Permitted to call Manna down from heaven

268) Eunice, who is referred to in Apostle Paul's letter in the Book of II Timothy, was Timothy's:

(See II Timothy Chapter 1 Verse 5)

A) Grandmother

B) Cousin

C) Sister

D) Daughter

E) Mother

269) Lois was:

(See II Timothy Chapter 1 Verse 5)
A) Peter's Mother

B) Paul's Mother

C) Paul's Grandmother

D) Timothy's Grandmother

E) Timothy's Sister-in-law

270) Apostle Paul's advice on marriage was evidently intended for:

(See I Corinthians Chapter 7 Verse 1-2; I Corinthians Chapter 1 Verse 2)
A) Only the Jewish Members of the church

B) The general public (Unbelievers)

C) Preachers, Deacons

D) Gentiles

E) All Members of the Church baptised, born-again, and have accepted Jesus Christ as Lord and Saviour

271) Apostle Paul wrote in the Book of Corinthians, "For it is better to marry," than to:

(See I Corinthians Chapter 7 Verse 8-9)

A) Burn with passion

B) Live in guilt

C) Be frustrated

D) Be depressed

E) Be a stalker

272) Apostle Paul declared that he did not judge himself because:

(See I Corinthians Chapter 4 Verse 3-4)

A) He considered himself better than Apostle Peter and the other Apostles

B) He changed his name from Saul to Paul and was therefore not to be judged

C) He was not present when Jesus Christ was betrayed by Judas Iscariot

D) It was a different part of his life when he persecuted the early church

E) It is the Lord, God Almighty, who judges

273) "Get thee behind me, Satan," said Jesus Christ to:

(See Matthew Chapter 16 Verse 23)

A) Judas Iscariot

B) Andrew

C) James

D) Satan (Himself)

E) Peter

274) Jesus Christ said that it is easier for a camel to go through the eye of a needle than for:

(See Matthew Chapter 19 Verse 24)

A) Any person to observe the Ten Commandments

B) A Sinner to beg forgiveness

C) The Prodigal Son to return home

D) A rich man to enter into the Kingdom of God

E) The Pharisees and Sadducees to claim that they were the righteous ones

275) David when he became king was:

(See II Samuel Chapter 5 Verse 4)

A) 30 years Old

B) A young shepherd boy

C) 35 years Old

D) 33 years Old

E) 45 years Old

276) In King David's administration, Jehoshaphat, the son of Ahilud, was a:

(See II Samuel Chapter 8 Verse 15)

A) Priest

B) Recorder

C) In charge of the Cherethites and the Pelethites

D) Commander-in-Chief over the army

E) Treasurer

277) After the death of King Saul:

(See II Samuel Chapter 3 Verse 1)

A) Jonathan and David became good friends

B) He married Michal

C) He killed Ishbosheth

D) He asked Abner to be Commander-in-Chief of the army

E) There was long conflict and clashes with the house of Saul and the house of David

278) When King David asked in the Book of II Samuel if there was still anyone alive from the house of Saul, he wanted to:

(See II Samuel Chapter 9 Verse 1)

A) Be ruthless to the house of Saul

B) Show kindness to Mephibosheth for Jonathan's sake

C) Take Michal who was promised to him by her father (King Saul) for a hundred Philistine Foreskins

D) Gather information for a funeral speech on Saul

E) To send the house of Saul into exile to prevent any mutiny or uprising

279) Upon his (King David's) re-ascension to the throne of ancient Israel, his ten concubines were:

(See II Samuel Chapter 20 Verse 3)

A) Released from where Absalom had kept them captive

B) Beheaded

C) Shut up in seclusion to the day of their death

D) Burnt alive

E) Sent into exile.

SECTION FIVE

ANSWER TRUE OR FALSE

280) Revelations is the last Book of the Bible. True or False.

281) Nebuchadnezzar II is an important character in the Book of Daniel. True or False.

282) In the Christian home, husbands are to love and cherish their wives. True or False.
(See Colossians Chapter 3 Verse 19)

283) Daniel was the only person out of the ancient Jewish Captives that obeyed God. True or False.
(See Daniel Chapter 1 Verse 6-7; 19-20)

284) The Kingdom of ancient Israel was split under King Solomon for serving false gods. True or False.
(See I Kings Chapter 11 Verse 13)

285) King Solomon served and worshipped God faithfully throughout his reign as King of the Unified Kingdom of ancient Israel. True or False.
(See I Kings Chapter 11 Verse 1-13)

286) Nebuchadnezzar II was the greatest king of the Chaldean dynasty of Babylonia, conquering ancient Syria, Palestine, and destroying the Temple of Jerusalem thus initiating the Babylonian Captivity of the ancient Jews. True or False.

(See Jeremiah Chapter 46 Verse 13; Daniel Chapter 4 Verse 30)

287) Zedekiah (also known as Mattaniah) reign ended in Nebuchadnezzar II destruction of Jerusalem in 597 BC (Before Christ). True or False.

(See Jeremiah Chapter 39 Verse 1-9)

288) Prophet Jeremiah was executed by Nebuchadnezzar II when he invaded Jerusalem. True or False.

(See Jeremiah Chapter 39 Verse 11-18)

289) Zedekiah was the last King of Judah. True or False.

290)Which of the Following Statements are True?

The Acts of Apostles can be seen as:

A) The death of The Apostles of Jesus Christ

B) The great exploits of Apostle Peter (Acts Chapter 1-Acts Chapter 12) and Apostle Paul (Acts Chapter 13-Acts Chapter 28) in propagating the Gospel of Jesus Christ to the Jewish and Gentile World

C) The death of Deacon Stephen

D) The decline of the Apostles

E) Restoring the Kingdom of David

291) Philip was one of the original Seven Deacons chosen in the church community in Jerusalem to care for the widows, as well as performing miracles in Samaria, and baptising the Ethiopian Eunuch. True or False.

292) Lying to the Holy Spirit cost Ananias and Sapphira their lives. True or False.

(See Acts of Apostles Chapter 5 Verse 1-11)

293) Saul who later became Apostle Paul (before his conversion) used to persecute some of the early disciples in the early church. True or False.

(See Acts of the Apostles Chapter 8 Verse 1-3)

294) Apostle Paul is considered as one of the most important figures in the Apostolic Age. True or False.

(See Acts of Apostle Chapter 13-Chapter 28)

295) Apostle Peter was the first Apostle to preach the Gospel of Jesus Christ to the Gentiles. True or False.

(See Acts of Apostles Chapter 10 Verse 1-8)

ANSWER A, B, C, D, OR E

296) "Upon this rock I will build my church," and "I will give to thee the keys of the kingdom of heaven," said Jesus Christ to:

(See Matthew Chapter 16 Verse 17-19)

A) Peter

B) James and John (The sons of Zebedee)

C) Andrew

D) Matthew

E) Judas Iscariot

297) Who is symbolically referred to as "the rose of Sharon"?:
(See Song of Solomon Chapter 2 Verse 1)

A) Jesus Christ

B King David

C) King Solomon

D) Bathsheba

E) Sarah

298) Ruth and Boaz were great grandparents of:
(See Ruth Chapter 4 Verse 13-17)

A) Joab

B) Jesus Christ

C) King David

D) King Solomon

E) Joshua

299) Which great Army Commander-in-Chief in the Bible
prayed for the Sun to stand still?
(See Joshua Chapter 10)

A) Abner

B) Naaman

C) Jehu

D) Joab

E) Joshua

300) Who advised King David against taking a census of Israel and Judah?

(See II Samuel Chapter 24 Verse 1-9)

A) Joab

B) Abishai

C) Prophet Nathan

D) Benaiah

E) Adonijah

301) "Rejoice not against me oh my enemy: when I fall, I shall arise; when I sit in darkness, the Lord shall be a light unto me," was spoken by whom?

(See Micah Chapter 7 Verse 8)

A) King David in the Book of Psalms

B) King Solomon in the Book of the Song of Solomon

C) Jesus Christ in the Sermon on the Mountain

D) Samson

E) Micah the Prophet

302) The Biblical quotation: "I will lift up my eyes to the hills from where comes my help, my help comes from the Lord, who made heaven and earth" can be found in the:

A) Book of Genesis

B) Book of Matthew

C) Book of Psalms

D) Book of Proverbs

E) Book of Lamentations

303) Who were described as the ancient Israelites' fiercest enemies in the Bible?

A) The Tuaregs

B) The Philistines

C) The Edomites

D) The Babylonians

E) The Syrians

304) Solomon was born to King David and Bathsheba in:

A) Rome

B) Egypt

C) Hebron

D) Bethlehem

E) Jerusalem

305) Which one of these individuals was not a son of King David?

A) Nathan

B) Amnon

C) Daniel

D) Joab

E) Shephatiah

306) Which one of these was not a wife of King David?

A) Rachel

B) Michal

C) Abigail

D) Ahinoam

E) Maacah (Daughter of Talmai King of Geshur)

307) Who uttered these words in the Bible? *"Now therefore, the sword shall never depart from your house, because you have despised me, and taken the wife of Uriah the Hittite to be your wife."*

(See II Samuel Chapter 12 Verse 10)

A) Prophet Elijah to Ahab

B) Prophet Nathan to David

C) Prophet Daniel to Nebuchadnezzar

D) Prophet Samuel to King Saul

E) None of the above

308) Prophet Ezra in the Bible was responsible for:

A) Getting his countrymen and women to return to God and prevent improper marriages

B) Return to idol worshipping

C) Returning his countrymen and women to Babylon

D) Stirring up a revolt amongst his people

E) None of the above

309) King Darius and Cyrus the Great gave the decree that:

A) The temple of God should be destroyed

B) The temple of God should be transferred

C) The temple of God should be looted

D) The temple of God should be re-named

E) The temple of God should be rebuilt for praise and worship

310) Both Prophet Ezra and Nehemiah:

A) Caused discord amongst the ancient Israelites

B) Were contemporaries focusing on rebuilding the walls and temple of Jerusalem (Ezra concentrating on the religious aspect and Nehemiah on the political aspect)

C) Were false Prophets

D) Wanted to overthrow the Persian Empire

E) None of the above

311) In the Bible, Achish was:

A) The King of Egypt

B) The King of Gath

C) The King of Benin

D) The King of Babylon

E) The King of Nineveh

312) Jacob's favourite child was:

(See Genesis Chapter 37 Verse 3)

A) Reuben

B) Dinah

C) Joseph

D) Solomon

E) Benjamin

313) Moses escaped from Egypt because:

A) He killed his fellow kinsmen

B) He killed an Amalekite

C) He killed a Philistine

D) He killed an Egyptian

E) He was a spy

314) In the Bible, a Milcom is a:

A) Sword

B) god

C) Machine

D) Coat

E) Locust

315) "The Lord is my light and my salvation" is:

A) Psalm 27

B) Psalm 23

C) Proverbs 4

D) Psalm 16

E) Psalm 1

316) "The voice of one crying in the wilderness" is that of:

A) Prophet Elijah

B) King Pharaoh

C) Prophet Jeremiah

D) Absalom

E) John the Baptist

317) Hope deferred makes the:

A) Soul sad

B) Soul vexed

C) Heart tough

D) Mind go insane

E) Heart sick

318) In the Book of Genesis, God created man out of:

A) Oxygen

B) Air

C) Mud

D) Dust

E) Clay

319) To be healed of his leprosy, The Syrian General Naaman was told by Prophet Elisha to dip himself seven times in:

A) The River Niger

B) The River Thames

C) The River Jordan

D) The Atlantic Ocean

E) The River Benue

320) In the Book of Genesis, it is described that it:

A) Rained for 40 days and 40 nights

B) Rained for 30 days and 30 nights

C) Rained for 20 days and 10 nights

D) Rained for 1 day

E) Rained 3 days

321) In the Book of Genesis, on the third day, God:

(See Genesis Chapter 1 Verse 11-13)

A) Created the whales and fish

B) Created Human beings

C) Said, "Let the earth bring forth grass"

D) Created cattle

E) Created none of the above

322) God created woman by:

(See Genesis Chapter 1 Verse 22-23)

A) Taking seven ribs out of Adam's side

B) Taking three ribs out of Adam's side

C) Taking two ribs out of Adam's side

D) Taking four ribs out of Adam's side

E) Taking one rib out of Adam's side

323) When the flood covered the earth in the Book of Genesis, Noah was:

(See Genesis Chapter_)

A) Six Hundred years old

B) Two Hundred years old

C) Four Hundred years old

D) Five Hundred years old

E) Ninety years old

324) Moab was:

(See Genesis Chapter 19 Verse 36-37)

A) Abraham's son

B) Isaac's brother

C) Lot's brother

D) Lot's son and grandson

E) Lot's nephew

325) Ishmael was the son of:

A) King David and Abigail

B) King David and Ahinoam

C) Abraham and Sarah

D) Abraham and Hagar

E) Elkanah and Peninnah

326) Which army commander in the Bible spent six months in exterminating the ancient Edomites?

A) Joab

B) Joshua

C) Amasa

D) Abner

E) Jehu

327) In the book of II Samuel, which of the following went down on a snowy day to chase a lion into a pit and killed it, and also subdued two Moabite giants?

A) Abishai

B) Jehu

C) Abner

D) Amasa

E) Benaiah

328) "God will provide" refers to how he provided Abraham with:
(See Genesis Chapter 22 Verse 8, 13)

A) A son

B) Wealth

C) Wisdom

D) Honour

E) A ram

329) Apostle Paul's instructions for younger widows was to:
(See I Timothy Chapter 5 Verse 11-15)

A) Have two wives

B) Remarry and have children

C) Never remarry

D) Blame God

E) Remarry but have no children

330) Which character in the Bible vanquished the ancient Philistines until their hand was too tired to lift their sword?

A) Joab

B) Benaiah

C) Jehu

D) Eleazar, son of Dodai

E) Abner

331) When was Julius Caesar assassinated?

A) In 44 B.C.E

B) In 44 A.D

C) In 27 B.C.E

D) In 17 A.D

E) In 16 C.E

332) What year was the ancient First Temple of Jerusalem destroyed?

A) 370 A.D

B) 1270 B.C.E

C) 586 B.C

D) 610 A.D

E) 586 A.D

333) The Second Temple of Jerusalem was destroyed because of:

A) Fire

B) An ongoing revolt against the Babylonians

C) An ongoing revolt against the Edomites

D) An ongoing revolt against Alexander the Great

E) An ongoing revolt against the Romans

334) Mention what year the Second Temple of Jerusalem was destroyed:

A) 50 C.E

B) 70 C.E

C) 100 A.D

D) 10 B.C

E) 69 A.D

335) Which of the following Roman characters had the first link binding to the New Testament of the Bible?

(See Luke Chapter 2 Verse 1-2)

A) Brutus

B) Mark Anthony

C) Bassanio

D) Octavian (also known as Augustus Caesar)

E) Lepidus

336) Who did Jesus Christ utter the following words to in the Bible: "I was sent only to help God's lost sheep – the people of Israel."

(See Matthew Chapter 15 Verse 21-28)

A) Martha

B) The woman with the issue of blood

C) A Pharisee

D) The Centurion

E) A Gentile Woman

337) When Jesus Christ said that "Indeed a greater than Solomon was here", who was He referring to?

A) Octavius Augustus Caesar

B) Prophet Isaiah

C) John the Baptist

D) Daniel

E) Jesus Christ (Himself)

338) Which of the following events are recorded first in the Book of Acts of Apostles in the Bible?

A) A lame man healed at the Gate of the temple Beautiful by Apostles Peter and John

B) The stoning of Deacon Stephen

C) The conversion of the Ethiopian Eunuch

D) The Coming of the Holy Spirit (Day of Pentecost) and Apostle Peter's Sermon

E) The conversion of Saul (later known as Paul)

339) Who converted and baptised the Ethiopian Eunuch in the Bible?

A) Philip the Deacon and Evangelist

B) Apostle Peter

C) Apostle James

D) Apostle Paul

E) John the Baptist

340) At Joppa, who did Apostle Peter restore to life?

(See Acts of Apostles Chapter 9 Verse 36-43)

A) Mary Magdalene

B) Martha

C) Dorcas

D) Dinah

E) Jarius' daughter

341) In the Book of Acts of Apostles, who is being referred to in the following statement: "He is a chosen vessel of mine to bear my name before Gentiles, kings, and for the children of Israel. For I will show him how many things he must suffer for my name's sake."

A) Jesus Christ

B) Apostle Peter

C) King David

D) Prophet Jeremiah

E) Apostle Paul

342) Which one of King David's Psalms in the Bible says the following: "I have been young and now am old; yet I have not seen the righteous forsaken nor his descendants begging bread."

A) Psalm 23 Verse 25

B) Psalm 37 Verse 25

C) Psalm 3 Verse 16

D) Psalm 40 Verse 22

E) Psalm 36 Verse 10

343) What year do historians record that King David ascended the throne of ancient Israel?

A) 960 A.D

B) 790 B.C.E

C) 1010 B.C.E

D) 874 A.D

E) 1010 A.D

344) In the New Testament, Jesus Christ was recorded to have been born during the time of:

A) Nebuchadnezzar II

B) During the time Prophet Isaiah

C) During the time of the destruction of the First Temple

D) During the time of Herod the Great and Octavius Augustus Caesar

E) During the time of Daniel

345) The Herodian Dynasty was a royal of the:

A) Sayfawa Descent

B) Judah Royal family

C) Idumaen Dynasty (Edomite descent)

D) Davidic Dynasty

E) Benjamin tribe

346) Antipater I, the Idumaen, was the founder of the:

A) Babylonian Empire

B) The Songhai Empire

C) The Herodian Dynasty

D) The Persian Empire

E) The Greek Empire

347) What was Belteshazzar's Jewish or Hebrew name?

A) Daniel

B) Nathan

C) Joshua

D) Abishai

E) Manasseh

348) Who uttered the following words: "Daniel, servant of the living God! Was your God, who you serve so faithfully, able to rescue you from the lions?"

A) King Saul to Daniel

B) Nebuchadnezzar to Daniel

C) King Cyrus to Daniel

D) Emperor Nero to Daniel

E) King Darius to Daniel

349) The story of the Prodigal Son in the Bible shows that the elder brother was:

A) Forgetful

B) Self-righteous

C) Bright

D) Hardworking

E) Honest

350) Which of these Emperors allowed the ancient Jews to return to their homeland after the fall of Babylonian Empire?

A) Cyrus the Great

B) Alexander the Great

C) Darius the Medes

D) Ahasuerus

E) Achish of Gath

351) Who was the founder of the Achaemenid Empire?

A) Alexander the Great

B) Mansa Musa

C) Cyrus the Great

D) Joab

E) Mark Anthony

352) Carchemish was an important location battle area in 605 B.C fought between the:

A) Philistines and Edomites

B) Babylonians and Egyptians
C) Syrians and the Anatolians

D) Ammonites and Israelites

E) Amalekites and Egyptians

353) What does Mesopotamia mean?

A) Between two rivers

B) Between two civilisations

C) Between two friends

D) Between two traitors

E) Between a rock and a hard place

354) Who overthrew the Persian Empire?

A) Napoleon Bonaparte

B) Judar Pasha

C) Alexander the Great

D) William the Conqueror

E) Mark Anthony

355) Which one of these Military Commanders was Jewish?

A) Judar Pasha

B) Lepidus

C) Mark Anthony

D) Joab

E) Sonni Ali

356) The four huge beasts described in the Book of Daniel represented:

A) The gap between the rich and poor

B) The decline of human civilisation

C) The four kingdoms that were to emerge on the earth (Babylonian, Medo-Persia, Greek, and Roman Empire)

D) The acceleration of the Industrial Revolution in Europe

E) The Scramble and Partition of West Africa

357) Which one of these prominent ancient African Rulers was the first to become a Christian and encourage the spread of Christianity in their empire?

A) Oba Ewuare the Great

B) Mai Idris Alooma

C) Sundiata Keita

D) Queen Aminat

E) Oba Esigie

358) Who died first out of the following followers or believers of Jesus Christ?

A) Stephen the Deacon

B) Judas Iscariot

C) James (the bother of John and son of Zebedee)

D) Apostle Peter

E) Apostle Paul

359) Which one of the following converted the English Bible into Yoruba?

A) Joseph Flavius

B) Ahmad Bin Fartuwa

C) Bishop Ajayi Crowther

D) King James

E) Jehoshaphat

360) Who was described as the 'Disciple to the Gentiles'?

A) Philip the Deacon and Evangelist

B) Stephen the Deacon

C) Apostle Paul

D) Apostle Andrew

E) Apostle Peter

361) Where were the followers of Jesus Christ first called Christians?

A) Cairo

B) Alexandria

C) Ziklag

D) Joppa

E) Antioch

362) Which disciple introduced Saul (who become Paul) to the rest of the disciples?

A) Matthias

B) Andrew

C) Barnabas

D) John (the brother of James)

E) Dorcas

363) The incident at Antioch was an Apostolic disagreement between:

A) Elijah and the False Prophets of Baal

B) Apostle Paul and Apostle Peter

C) King David and Joab (Commander of Army of Israel)

D) Deacon Stephen the Sanhedrin Council

E) Paul and Barnabas

364) Who were the Sanhedrin?

A) The Supreme Legal Court of the Europeans

B) The Supreme Legal Court of the Jewish Elders

C) The Supreme Court of Julius Caesar

D) King Solomon's Supreme Court

E) Horns of the alter

365) Which Disciple, Follower, or Apostle of Jesus Christ denounced their listeners as "stiff-necked" people who, just as their ancestors had done, resist the Holy Spirit?

A) Apostle Andrew

B) John the Baptist

C) Apostle Thomas

D) Philip, the Deacon and Evangelist

E) Stephen, the Deacon

366) Who was described as the Law Giver to the ancient Israelites in the Bible?

A) Moses

B) Prophet Elisha

C) King David

D) Abraham

E) Noah

367) Apostle Peter's address to the Jerusalem Council in Acts of Apostle Chapter 15 Verse 7-11 was to:

A) Add more conflict and disagreement over the issue of Circumcision

B) Create Christians that followed Peter and Christians that followed Paul

C) Resolve the issue over the conflict of Circumcision

D) Advocate for the return of the Davidic Dynasty

E) Stay silent over the matter

368) What date, according to historic sources, did the Davidic Dynasty come to an end?

A) 612 B.C.E

B) 750 B.C.E

C) 450 A.D

D) 437 A.D

E) 586 B.C.E

369) King David in the Book of Psalms Chapter 8 Verse 5 praises God for making us (Human beings)"

A) Equal to Angels

B) A little lower than Angels

C) Better than Angels

D) To pray to Angels

E) To serve Angels

370) In Psalm 23, King David says: "The Lord is ... "

A) My Shepherd

B) My Stranger

C) My Scientist

D) My Historian

E) My Timekeeper

371) Uzziah was a king of:

A) Persian Empire

B) Assyrian Empire

C) Judah (Davidic Line)

D) Babylonian Empire

E) Roman Empire

372) Ahaz was described as a:

A) Wicked King of Israel

B) Wicked King of Judah

C) Good King of Israel

D) Good King of the Unified Kingdom of Israel

E) Bad King of the Unified Kingdom of Israel

373) Who conquered the Northern Kingdom of Israel in 722 B.C.E?

A) The Roman Empire

B) The Tuaregs

C) The Hittie Empire

D) The Neo-Assyrian Empire

E) The Mali Empire

374) Which Foreign King led the attack on the Northern Kingdom of Israel?

A) Shalmaneser

B) Alexander the Great

C) Askia the Great

D) Cyrus the Great

E) Juda Pasha

375) What King did God extend their life by 15 years?

A) King Ahaz

B) King Ahab

C) King Rehoboam

D) King Hezekiah

E) King Solomon

376) The ancient Israelites were in bondage in ancient Egypt for:

A) 660 years

B) 223 years

C) 430 years

D) 550 years

E) 780 years

377) In the new Jerusalem referred to in Revelation Chapter 21 Verse 4 of the Bible, there will be no more:

A) Anguish

B) Sadness

C) Crying

D) Depression

E) Death, Sorrow, Crying, Pain

378) Which one of these Jewish individuals did not live during the Neo-Assyrian Ancient Period?

A) Joab

B) Ahaz

C) Hezekiah

D) Jeremiah

E) Jonah

379) "Get thee behind me, Satan" is what Jesus said to:

A) Andrew

B) Lucifer

C) Judas Iscariot

D) Thomas

E) Peter

380)Who is Queen Athaliah in the Bible?

A) King Rehoboam's daughter

B) Jacob's daughter

C) King Ahab's daughter

D) Esau's daughter

E) King Solomon's daughter

381) Who was responsible for exterminating the house of Ahab?

A) Mai Idris Alooma

B) Joab (Commander of Army over all of the 12 tribes of Israel)

C) Benaiah (Commander of the Cherethites and the

Pelethites)

D) Mark Anthony

E) Jehu

382) The reign of Jehu was marked by the battle of:

A) Gilboa

B) Tondibi

C) Jericho

D) Ramoth-Gilead

E) Refidim

383) Jehu was the son of:

A) King David

B) King Hezekiah

C) Prophet Elisha

D King Rehoboam

E) King Jehoshaphat

384) Which one of these Jewish Biblical heroes is described in the Bible to have carried away the Philistines Gates of Gaza?

A) Joab

B) Samson

C) David

D) Joshua

E) Deborah

385) In the Bible, who uttered these words?: "How can you say, 'I love you', when your heart is not with me? You have deceived me these three times and have not told me where your great strength lies."

A) Potiphar to Joseph

B) Queen (Makeda) Sheba to King Solomon

C) Abigail to King David

D) Queen Vashti to King Ahasuerus

E) Delilah to Samson

ANSWER TRUE OR FALSE TO THE FOLLOWING STATEMENTS

386) Jesus Christ said He came only to the "Lost House of Israel."

387) Adam and Eve remained in the Garden of Eden after they disobeyed God.

388) The death of all the Apostles are recorded in the Bible.

389) Athaliah was a tyrannical usurper of the throne of Judah.

390) Esther was a Queen of the Achaemenid Empire.

391) King David's forty-year reign of the Unified Kingdom of Ancient Israel was referred to as Israel's "Golden Age".

392) Athaliah epitomised all the wickedness of her infamous parents (King Ahab and Queen Jezebel) and transferred the toxin of idolatry into Judah.

393) Daniel was a king in the ancient Neo-Babylonian Empire.

394) Esau and Jacob were fraternal twins.

395) The wicked and treacherous Jezebel was thrown from the window by her eunuchs (on the command of Jehu), where she died instantly, and the dogs ate the remains of her body.

396) Cain got away with killing his brother, Abel.

397) Apostle Paul said in the Book of Romans that: "If it is possible, as much as depends on you, live at peace with everyone."

398) Apostle Paul says that every soul should be resistant to the governing authorities.

399) King Solomon, in the Book of Proverbs, says: "A soft answer turns away wrath, but harsh words stir up anger."

400) Jesus Christ said to a rich man in the Synoptic Gospels that it was easier for a camel to go through the eye of a needle than a rich man to enter the Kingdom of God.

ANSWER A, B, C, D or E

401) Why was God displeased with King David?

A) He (David) arranged for a soldier that served in his army to be killed and then took his wife

B) He (David) married many wives and Concubines

C) He (David) did not fully appreciate the military feats of Joab, his Army Commander

D) He (David) was not good at training his children

E) He (David) was at constant war with the house of his predecessor

402) What Empire destroyed the Second Temple?

A) The Mali Empire

B) The British Empire

C) The Persian Empire

D) The Roman Empire

E) The Benin Empire

403) In which year was the Second Temple destroyed?

A) 50 C.E

B) 45 A.D

C) 70 C.E

D) 80 C.E

E) 70 A.D

404) What was the Bar Kokhba Revolt?

A) A revolt of Judah against the Philistines

B) A revolt of Judah against the Neo-Assyrian Empire

C) A revolt of Judah against the Greek Empire

D) A revolt of Judah against the Neo-Babylonian Empire

E) A revolt of Judah against the Roman Empire

405) Under what Roman Emperor was first Jewish-Roman War or Great Revolt?

A) Julius Caesar

B) Mark Anthony

C) Nero

D) Octavius Augustus Caesar

D) Marcus Aemilius Lepidus

406) Who was Titus Flavius Josephus?

A) An Event Recorder in King David's Administration

B) A Wise Man in Babylon

C) A Jewish Priest, Scholar, and Historian who wrote on Early Jewish History as well as the Jewish-Roman Conflicts

D) An administrator in Babylon

E) A Scholar from Tripoli

407) What does the title 'Augustus' mean?

A) Revered, Majestic, Venerable

B) Holy One

C) Lord

D) Pleasant

E) Anointed One

408) Who was the Roman Emperor during Jesus Christ's birth?

A) Nero

B) Octavius Augustus Caesar

C) Tiberus Caesar

D) Mark Anthony

E) Lepidus

409) What year did the Roman Empire invade Britain?

A) 60 A.D

B) 75 B.C

C) 26 A.D

D) 43 A.D

E) 40 B.C

410) In the Bible, who was turned into a Pillar of Salt?

A) The Egyptians

B) Lot's Wife

C) Nebuchadnezzar II

D) Naaman

E) Absalom

411) Why was God angry with King Solomon?

A) He (Solomon) did not fully follow God like his great father King David had turned to Idolatry

B) He (Solomon) married too many wives

C) He (Solomon) had become a dictator

D) He (Solomon) ran into the sunset with the Queen of Sheba

E) He (Solomon) married a daughter of Pharaoh of Egypt

412) What did Jesus Christ do when Satan asked him to prove himself as the Son of God?

A) Overcame Satan with the written Word of God

B) Ignored Satan

C) Became afraid of Satan

D) Through himself off the Pinnacle of the Temple

E) Asked Satan to repent

413) According to Historical Church traditional, Apostle Peter was martyred by:

A) Being thrown to the Lions

B) Whipped to death

C) Crucified upside down on an X-Shaped Cross

D) Beheaded

E) Drowned

414) What year was Apostle Paul martyred?

A) 70 B.C

B) 64 A.D

C) 50 B.C.E

D) 45 A.D

E) 64 B.C

415) Mary Magdalene was known for:

A) Gossiping

B) Partying

C) Being hostile

D) Anointing Jesus Christ's Feet with Oil

E) Sowing a garment of many colours for Jesus Christ

416) Who are known as the Patriarchs in the Bible?

A) King Saul, King David, King Solomon

B) Abraham, Isaac, and Jacob

C) Jacob, Esau, and Laban

D) Ashael, Abishai, and Joab

E) Sarah, Hannah, and Elizabeth

417) Jacob's first born was:

A) Joseph

B) Benjamin

C) Saul

D) Lot

E) Reuben

418) Who was Jacob's favourite son:
A) Judah

B) Reuben

C) Dan

D) Simeon

E) Joseph

419) Who said, "If it possible, let this cup pass from me!" in the Garden of Gethsemane?

A) Jesus Christ

B) Peter

C) James

D) John

E) Andrew

420) Golgotha is where Jesus Christ:
A) Was Resurrected

B) Was tempted by Satan

C) Turned water into wine

D) Was crucified

E) Preached

421) How many Lepers did Jesus Christ Heal in Luke Chapter 17 Verse 11-19?

A) 7

B) 10

C) 5

D) 1

E) 0

422) How many Lepers went back to Jesus Christ to express their appreciation?

A) 5

B) 10

C) 1

D) None

E) 6

423) What was the origin of the Leper that came back to thank Jesus Christ?

A) African

B) Roman

C) British

D) Jew

E) Samaritan

424) When Jesus Christ said to his agitators, "Destroy this temple, and in three days I will raise it up," what was He (Jesus Christ) referring to?

A) The First Temple

B) The Dynasty of King David

C) The First Roman Triumvirate

D) His own (Jesus Christ) Death, Burial, and Resurrection

E) The Rise, Decline, and Fall of the Songhai Empire

425) What key theme can be learnt from the account of Jesus Christ healing the Lepers in the Book of Luke in the Bible?

A) We should be thankful and show appreciation when we receive a gift

B) Show why we should be blessed first

C) Expecting that the world owes us something

D) Show how faithful we are

E) Be Critical

SECTION SIX

USEFUL
CHRISTIAN/BIBLICAL/HISTORIC
TERMINOLOGY/ACRONYMS

1) Achaemenid Empire was known as the first Persian. It was an ancient Iranian Empire based in Western Asia founded by Cyrus the Great. From its extent from the Balkans and Eastern Europe proper in the west to the Indus Valley in the East (Asia), it was more enormous than any empire in history, spreading over 5. 5 million kilometres. It incorporated people of various different origins and faiths. It was also renowned for its accomplishing of a centralised, bureaucratic administration through the satraps.

(See Biblical references to satraps in Daniel Chapter 3 Verse 2-3, and Daniel Chapter 6)

2) A.D. means Anno Domini, literally translated as Year of Our Lord.

3) Alexander III of Macedonia was commonly known as Alexander the Great. He was a member of the Argead Dynasty and succeeded his father Philip II. He spent most of his career on unprecedented military campaigns through Western Asia (Anatolia, Arabian Peninsula, Iran, Levant, and Mesopotamia). By the age of thirty he had created one of the largest empires of the ancient world, stretching from Greece

to North-western India. He was undefeated in battle and is widely considered as one of history's most successful military commanders.

4) Ancient of Near East is referred to or considered as one of the cradles of Civilisation.

5) Akkadian Empire was the first ancient empire in Mesopotamia. The empire consolidated the Akkadian and Sumerian People under one dominion. The Akkadian Empire reached its apogee between the twenty-second and twenty-fourth century BC under Sargon Akkad, its founder. After the decline of the Akkadian Empire, Mesopotamia fused into two main Akkadian-speaking entities: ancient Assyria and ancient Babylonia.

6) Antioch: This Greek City was founded towards the end of the fourth century BC by Seleucus I Nicator, one of Alexander the Great's Generals. Antioch was also known as "the cradle of Christianity" as a result of its longevity and the important role it has played in the rise of Hellenistic Judaism and early Christianity.

7) Apostle: Can be defined as an individual who has the assignment to impart an important message or teaching to others. The original twelve disciples later became known as apostles (in the Book of Acts of Apostles) when they went to uttermost ends of the earth to preach the Gospel of Jesus Christ.

8) Apostolic Age: This is named after the Apostles and their various missionary work. It holds a significant place in Christian tradition. The main source of tradition of the Apostolic Age is the Acts of Apostles. The earliest followers

of Jesus Christ were apocalyptic Jewish Christians. The early Christians were predominately Ebionites and the early Christian Community in Jerusalem was led by James, the brother of Jesus Christ. Antioch was the place where the Apostles were first called Christians. Apostle Peter and Apostle Paul were two of the greatest assets during the Apostolic Age of the early Church in the first century. (See the exploits of Apostle Peter in Acts Chapter 1-12 and Apostle Paul in Acts Chapter 13-28)

9) Atonement in Judaism: This is the process whereby a transgression or sin is pardoned or forgiven.

10) Atonement in Christianity: In Christianity, salvation is the saving or redeeming of human beings from death and separation from God by Jesus Christ's death and resurrection. Jesus Christ came to save the world, not to condemn it, and we see this in his crucifixion and resurrection.

11) B.C. means Before Christ

12) B.C.E. means Before Common Era

13) Bronze Age: It is the historical period dominated with the use of Bronze. The Bronze Age was from 3000-1200 BC.

14) Christian theology: This is the theology of Christian belief and practice. Such study is based on text from the Old Testament and the New Testament, as well as Christian tradition.

15) Dark Ages: This is a historical period referring to the Middle Ages (5th-15th Century) that affirmed a demographic, cultural, and economic deterioration that occurred in Western Europe after the demise of the Roman Empire.

16) David: He was one of the eight sons of Jesse and from the Israel tribe of Judah, Bethlehem, and Israel's greatest ever King.

17) Deacon: A Deacon is a member of the Diaconate, a position in the Christian Church. Denominational Churches such as the Catholic Church, Oriental Orthodox Church, the Eastern Orthodox Church, and the Anglican Church see the Diaconate as part of the clerical state. Stephen in the Book of Acts of Apostles (See Acts of Apostles Chapter 6) was one of the first Deacons in the early church. A biblical description of the qualities that a Deacon should adhere to can be found in the Book of Timothy.

(See I Timothy Chapter 3 Verse 8-13)

18) Deity: Jesus Christ is described in the Bible as "Eternal", "Omnipresent", (Present Everywhere) "Omniscient", (All Knowing) and "Omnipotent" (Unlimited Power). In the Holy Scriptures of the Bible, Jesus Christ himself also claimed Deity by teaching that He was equal with God and that whoever knows him knows God, to receive him was to receive God, to obey his commandments was to obey God; to hate him was to hate God.

19) Disciple: A follower, pupil, student, or learner. Jesus Christ had twelve original disciples when he carried out his ministry on earth.

20) Early Church: The Early Church spread from the Eastern Mediterranean to throughout the Roman Empire and beyond to parts of Europe and Africa. The early followers of Christianity were first the Jews (an ethnoreligious group and a nation emerging from the Israelites and Hebrews of historical Israel and Judah).

21) Ebionites: A Jewish Christian Sect or Movement that existed during the early Christian First Century Era. They regarded Jesus Christ of Nazareth as the Messiah but did not hold firmly to the belief of his divinity and virgin birth and insisted on the continued following of the Jewish Law and Rites.

22) Emmanuel: means God is with us.

23) The Ethiopian Eunuch: He was the first African convert to Christianity in the Book of Acts of Apostles. His conversion is one of the outstanding converts in The Acts of Apostles. The Eunuch was returning from worship at Jerusalem and going home. He was sitting in his chariot reading the Book of Isaiah. He was reading Isaiah Chapter 53 Verse 7-8. Philip asked the Eunuch whether he understood what he was reading. The Eunuch replied that he needed a teacher to teach him. Philip then explained the scripture to him and told him about Jesus Christ. The Eunuch believed and asked to be baptised by Philip. When they reached a river, Philip baptised the Eunuch.

24) Evangelism: This is the commitment or pledge to act by publicly preaching the Gospel message of Jesus Christ to new converts. Christians who specialise in evangelism work are called evangelists or missionaries.

25) Fishers of Men: Jesus Christ said to Simon Peter, Andrew (who were brothers), James and John (were also brothers and Sons of Zebedee) while they were casting a net into the sea because they were originally fishermen. Jesus said to them: "Follow me and I will make you fishers of men." (See Matthew Chapter 4 Verse 19) They immediately left their fishing nets and followed Jesus Christ.

26) Gilboa (Mount): Where King Saul led his last battle charge against arch-enemies the Philistines at the battle of Gilboa. The battle ends where King Saul takes his life by falling on his own sword to avoid capture and his sons are killed in the battle. King-in-waiting (David) hears about the tragedy after the battle and then pronounces a curse on the mountain (See II Samuel Chapter 1 Verse 17-27)

27) Golden Age: Under the reign of Israel's greatest king, Israel entered what historian's call a "golden age". King David was an emperor that served and obeyed God's commandments and with that came military success. He was also blessed with a talented resourceful and courageous army commander (Joab) who helped make this possible. Historians put King's David reign at 1010-970 BCE.

(See I Samuel, II Samuel, and I Chronicles for his Religious, Military, Political, and diplomatic achievements)

28) Greco-Rome Period: This was from 332 BC-395 AD. It is a form of comprising the interlocking civilisations of ancient Greece and ancient Rome. The Persians (now known as Iran) were defeated by the Greek Conqueror Alexander the Great who occupied Egypt and established a new capital in Alexandria.

29) Greek – Septuagint: This is the converting of books from Hebrew into Greek.

30) Halakha: Is a collective body of Jewish religious laws from the written Oral Torah. Halakha is based on the Biblical Commandments (Mitzvot), some differences in the Halakha observation could be amongst some different Jewish communities such as: Ashkenazi, Mizrahi, Sephardi, Yemenite, Ethiopian, and other Jewish Communities that live separately.

31) Hellenistic-Judaism: was where Jewish Religious Culture and elements of Greece culture merged. Hellenistic-Judaism existed in Jerusalem during the Second Temple period where there were conflicts between the Hellenisers and the Judaisers.

32) Jehovah: Is one of the seven names that God our creator and heavenly father is known by in the Holy Bible. Jehovah is also the proper name that they address God as in the Hebrew Bible. Other names that God is known by are: King of Kings, Lord of Lords, Lord of Hosts. Others names that God is known by in Christian worship settings are: Ancient of Days, Abba Father, Elohim, El-Shaddai, Yahweh, and Adonai.

33) Jebusites: In the Book of Joshua and II Samuel Chapter 5 Verse 6, were a Canaanite tribe that occupied Jerusalem before they were conquered by Joshua and finally by David when he was King. Joab, David's nephew and later Commander-in-Chief, led the assault on the Jebusites by sneaking up a Watershaft and launching an attack from within the fortress.

34) Joab: He was the nephew of King David and probably Israel's greatest ever army Commander General. He came to prominence at the battle of the Gibeon Pool (defeating Abner his arch-enemy and rival, as well as later assassinating him) who was the Commander General under King Saul during the civil war between the House of David and House of Saul. He (Joab) led the Commando assault against the Jebusites by sneaking through the Watershaft (Warren's Watershaft) and launched an attack from inside to take the fortress for King David. He went onto accomplish further military accomplishments on the battlefield by defeating the Philistines, the Syrians, the Moabites, the Ammonites, and the Edomites. He was one of the very few men that could stand up to King David, and his men had great trust and loyalty in him. Uriah, one of his soldiers, even called him 'lord'. Joab never lost a battle in his entire life.

(Refer to II Samuel for more on Joab)

35) Judaism: Is an ethnic religion that composes of the religious, cultural, and legal tradition of the Jewish People. Judaism is considered by religious or God-fearing Jews to be the expression of the covenant that God established with the ancient children of Israel. The Torah is part of the larger text known as the Tanakh, also known as the Hebrew Bible.

36) Levant: This is a vast area in the Eastern Mediterranean of West Asia. It includes the present-day Syria, Lebanon, Jordan, Israel, Palestine, Turkey, and the Euphrates.

37) Philistines: The ancient Philistines in the Bible attempted to attack ancient Egypt but were forced to retreat by Ramses III. They were inhabitants that dwelt in Canaan in the 12th Century when they were also forced to retreat to Mesopotamia by Nebuchadnezzar II. They were also called the Sea People. The Philistines under King Abimelech that

Abraham encountered (see Genesis Chapter 21 Verse 22 – 34) were more cordial compared to the Philistines in the Book of Judges, I Samuel, and II Samuel where they were ruled by warlords and their relationship with ancient Israel was more hostile. They were ancient Israel's arch most dangerous enemies in the Bible.

38) Rabbi: Is a Spiritual leader or Religious Teacher in Judaism.

39) Realpolitik: A political or governmental system not based on religion, ethic, doctrines, or morals but rather on realistic or practical ideas.

40) Tanaka: Is the canonical collection of the Hebrew Scriptures in the Old Testament. This is known as the Hebrew Bible. It can also be known as the Mikra. The text is in Biblical Hebrew and Biblical Aramaic. It is the twenty-four books of the Hebrew Bible.

41) Torah: The Torah or Pentateuch is the first Five Books of Moses in the Hebrew Christian Bible of the Old Testament.

42) Ziklag: This was a city mentioned in the Bible that was owned by the ancient Philistines. Achish, the Philistine ruler, gave the city to David to stay in with his family and warriors when he was on the run from King Saul. When David and his warriors were out on a raid the city was burnt down by the Amalekites who had also taken away their families.

(See I Samuel Chapter 30)

SECTION SEVEN

GALLERY

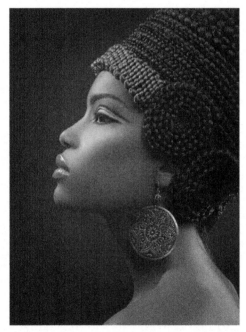

A portrait of Queen Sheba, courtesy of Fulaba.

A portrait picture of King Solomon's Temple. Built by Phoenician architects, described in I Kings Chapter 6 Verse 7 of the Bible, which was typical of temples of the region in the 10th Century.

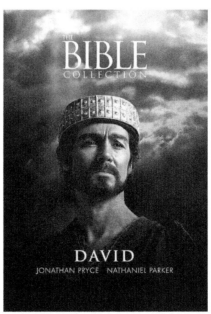

A portrait Picture of King David from the TV Movie Boxset played wonderfully by Nathaniel Parker.

Portrait Image of Joab, courtesy of Quodra

Joab was the son of Zeruiah (King David's half-sister). Joab was one of the greatest Commanders in the history of the Old Testament in the Bible. He led the assault on the Jebusites (Jerusalem) and was rewarded for it by King David (his uncle) when he was promoted to Commander-in-Chief of the army.

David Olawale Ayinde as Balthazar in the outdoor theatre 2016 production 'The Life of Jesus Christ' at Wintershall, Guilford.

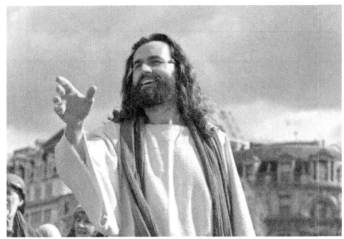

Courtesy Portrait of James Burke-Dunsmore

James Burke-Dunsmore plays Jesus Christ in the Re-enactment of The Passion and Life of Jesus Christ. James Burke-Dunsmore is one of the best actors to play Jesus Christ.

David Olawale Ayinde (Sitting 2nd from left) playing Apostle Thaddaeus in the Last Supper scene with James Burke-Dunsmore as Jesus Christ in the Re-enactment of The Passion of Jesus Christ.

Courtesy Portrait Picture of Victor Mature (Samson) and Hedy Lamarr in Cecil B. Demille's 'Samson and Delilah'.

Courtesy Portrait of Henry Wills, George Saunders, Hedy Lamarr, Angela Lansbury, Henry Wilcoxon, and Victor Mature in Cecil B. Demille's 'Samson and Delilah'.

Courtesy Picture of Queen Esther in the Bible by Karen Showell. Esther, also known as Hadassah (her Jewish name), was the queen of Persia. On becoming Queen, she performed a marvellous act of courage by preventing the destruction of her people (The Israelites) from the hands of one wicked Haman.

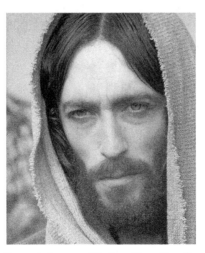

Courtesy Portrait Image of Robert Powell as Jesus Christ. (1977 TV Miniseries)

Courtesy Portrait of Robert Powell as Jesus Christ of Nazareth. Powell was amazing in the title role with an excellent supporting cast. (Jesus Christ of Nazareth, 1977 TV Mini Series)

Courtesy Image of Joseph fleeing from Portiphar's wife in the Bible.

A courtesy Portrait of The Mountain of Transfiguration. Moses represents the Law (Left), Jesus Christ, The Messiah (Centre), Elijah (Right) represents The Prophets, and the Disciples: Peter (Simon Peter), James and John

Courtesy Portrait of Ruth in the Bible by Francesco Hayes (1853).

SECTION EIGHT

ANSWERS TO QUESTIONS

1) Answer: The first book of the Bible in the Book of Genesis. It is known as the first Book of Moses.

2) Answer: The Bible consists of 66 Books. The Old Testament contains 39 Books. The New Testament contains 27 Books.

3) Answer: The Book of Malachi is found in the Book of the Old Testament. Malachi is the last Book in the Old Testament.

4) Answer: Psalm 23 was written by David who went on to be King David, ancient Israel's greatest ever king. David grew up and looked after his father's (Jesse) sheep but liked the metaphor of seeing God as his shepherd. The role of a shepherd is to ensure that the sheep are nourished and well looked after. Psalm 23 is one of the most popular Psalms in the Bible, revered by both Jews and Christians. (Refer to Psalm 23)

5) Answer: The disciples that accompanied Jesus Christ to the Mountain of Transfiguration were Peter (Simeon Peter),

James, and John. Refer to Matthew Chapter 17 Verse 1-9 for the full story of the transfiguration of Jesus Christ.

6) Answer: Jacob's first wife was Leah who bore him seven children (six sons and one daughter). Refer to Genesis Chapter 35 Verse 23-26 for brief story on Jacob's children.

7) Answer: Bilhah was Rachel's (Jacob's second wife's) Handmaid, she gave birth to sons Dan and Naphtali when Rachel gave Bilhah to Jacob to bear children. Refer to Genesis Chapter 30 Verse 3-7 for brief story.

8) Answer: Gad and Asher's mother is Zilpah. She was Leah's Handmaid. Leah gave Zilpah to Jacob who bore two sons called Gad and Asher. Refer to Genesis Chapter 30 Verse 9-13 for brief story.

9) Answer: Rachel, Jacob's second wife, gave birth to Joseph and Benjamin. Although Rachel does not live long enough to see the eventual destiny of her two children. God blesses both of them. We learn from the Bible how Joseph becomes a Prime Minster in Egypt (second in command after the Pharaoh), and ancient Israel's first king from the Unified Kingdom of Israel came from the tribe of Benjamin (King Saul).

10) Answer: God called Samuel three times before he (Samuel) answered. Samuel was a young boy in the care of the Prophet Eli. Hannah, Samuel's mother, vowed to dedicate him to God after he was born; she therefore brought him into the service of Eli. Refer to 1 Samuel Chapter 3 Verse 1-22 for the brief story on the Call of Samuel.

11) Answer: The three known Nazarites mentioned in the Bible are: Samson, Samuel, and John the Baptist. Refer to the Law of the Nazarite Numbers Chapter 6 Verse 1-21. Also see Judges Chapter 13 Verse 5 for Samson; 1 Samuel Chapter 1 Verse 11 for Samuel, and Luke Chapter 1 Verse 13-15.

12) Answer: The reason why God was more pleased with Abel's sacrifice than Cain's is because Abel had a heart and desire to give God the best. Abel was a Keeper of Sheep and Cain was a Farmer that turns over the ground. Abel brought the first-born of his flock of sheep. The best sheep in his flock. This is what blessed God and made his sacrifice more pleasing to God over his brother Cain. (Refer to Genesis Chapter 4 Verse 2-15 for brief story on Cain and Abel.)

13) Answer: The name of King David's sisters mentioned in the Bible were Zeruiah and Abigail. Also note that this Abigail is not the same Abigail that David took to become one of his wives. (Refer to 1 Samuel 25 Verse 2-42 to see full story) (Also see 2 Samuel Chapter 17 Verse 25, and 1 Chronicles Chapter 2 Verse 13-16)

14) Answer: King David's mother was Nitzevet and his father was Jesse. Jesse is the only person mentioned in the Bible. (Refer to I Samuel Chapter 16 Verse 2-16)

15) Answer: Ruth was a Moabite before converting to Judaism. (Refer to Ruth Chapter 1 Verse 16-22 to see a brief story on Ruth) Ruth is also amongst the five women named in the genealogy of Jesus Christ found in the Gospel Book of Matthew alongside Tamar, Rahab, wife of Uriah (Bathsheba), and Mary (the Mother of Jesus Christ). Refer to The Gospel Book of Matthew Chapter 1 Verse 1-17 for The Genealogy of Jesus Christ.

16) Answer: Absalom was King David's third son who was born to him in Hebron. His mother's name was Maacah. Absalom killed his half-brother Amnon for raping his sister Tamar. Absalom waited two years to avenge his sister's ordeal by instructing his servants to kill a drunken Amnon at a feast to which he (Absalom) invited all the King's sons. (Refer to 2 Samuel Chapter 13 for full story)

17) Answer: King Saul was jealous of David for the following reasons:

A) The women of Israel esteemed David above King Saul after David had killed the Philistine giant, Goliath. The women sang to each other, "Saul has killed his thousands, and David his ten thousands". This saying displeased King Saul. "They have given David honour for ten thousands, but for me only thousands. Now what more can he have but to be king?" King Saul was jealous and did not trust David from that day on. (Refer to 1 Samuel Chapter 18 Verse 5-9)

B) King Saul was jealous of David because the presence of God had left him (Saul) and was now with David.

C) King Saul was jealous because David conducted himself in a wise manner.

D) King Saul was also jealous because David was successful on whatever military raid he was sent on and Israel and Judah loved him as a result of it. (Refer to 1 Samuel Chapter 18 Verse 10-16)

18) Answer: Joab was the son of Zeruiah, a sister of King David. His father's name was Seraiah. Like his uncle, King David, Joab was a great warrior. After successfully leading the assault on the impregnable fortress of Mount Zion and capturing it, he was promoted to Commander-in-Chief of the army of the Unified Kingdom of Israel (Israel and Judah). Refer to 1 Chronicles Chapter 11 Verse 4-8 and 1 Chronicles

Chapter 27 Verse 34.

19) Answer: The Book of Exodus is the Second Book found in the Old Testament. It can also be referred to as the Second Book of Moses.

20) Answer: Five of King David's known wives in the Bible are: Ahinoam of Jezreel, Abigail from Carmel, Maacah from Talmai. Haggith, and Bathsheba. Ahinoam was the mother of Amnon, Abigail was the mother of Daniel, Maacah was the mother of Absalom, Haggith was the mother of Adonijah, and Bathsheba was the mother of Solomon. (Refer to 1 Chronicles Chapter 3 Verse 1-9 for the Descendants of King David.)

21) Answer: The names of Noah's children in the Bible were: Shem, Ham, and Japheth.

22) Answer: The Flood lasted for forty days. (Refer to Genesis Chapter 7 Verse 17-24 for brief story on the Flood)

23) Answer: Esau was the first born of Isaac and Rebekah. He was the elder twin brother of Jacob, and his grandparents were Abraham and Sarah. Esau was the progenitor (ancestor) of the Edomites.

24) Answer: Jacob who deceitfully stole his brother Esau's birthright by pretending to be Esau is what led to the feud between them. The feud had lasting consequences through to their descendants because of Jacob's deception. This conflict was paralleled by the affection the parents had for their favoured children. Isaac, who had a taste for wild game, loved

Esau, and Rebekah loved Jacob because he was simple and easy-going. (Refer to Genesis Chapter 25 Verse 28)

Before they were born, Rebekah was foretold by God that she would have two children that would struggle with each other insider her womb, and that the older brother would end up serving the younger brother. (Refer to Genesis Chapter 25 Verse 22-23)

We learn that in Genesis Chapter 25 Verse 26 that Jacob was grasping the heel of Esau as if he was trying to pull Esau back into their mother's womb so that he could be firstborn.

25) Answer: The Jebusites, according to the Book of Joshua in the Old Testament of the Bible, were a Canaanite tribe that occupied Jerusalem before the conquest by Joshua (Refer to Joshua Chapter 11 Verse 3, and Chapter 12 Verse 10), and followed up later by King David. King David wanted to take control of the city. The Jebusites challenged his attempt to do so. The Jebusites were a formidable force in Canaan. They mocked and gloated at King David and told him that their blind and lame would be more than a match for him and his army. David eventually was able to conquer the city by a surprise attack led by Joab. (Refer to 2 Samuel Chapter 5 Verse 6-9, 1 Chronicles Chapter 11 Verse 4-9)

26) Answer: Moses means "for I drew him out of the water" or "out of the Nile". According to the Old Testament book of the Bible, Moses was born when the ancient Jewish People (The Israelites) were enslaved by the ancient Egyptians. The Pharaoh had made a decree that all Hebrew boys be drowned in the River Nile, but Moses' mother placed him in a basket in the bulrushes by the Riverbank where the baby was found and adopted by Pharaoh's daughter and raised as an Egyptian. (Refer to Exodus Chapter 2 Verse 10 for the brief story of the birth of Moses.)

27) Answer: Jacob liked Joseph more than his other sons for the following reasons:

Reuben, who was Jacob's first born, had brought disgrace on the family through his sexual indiscretions with one of father's (Jacob) concubines. (Refer to Genesis Chapter 35 Verse 22 for brief story.) This resulted in him not only losing his father's respect but also his birthright as the first-born son. Jacob exercised his choice by appointing Joseph has heir to succeed him.

Another reason why Jacob liked Joseph more than his other sons was when his sons had brought shame to him after causing arson to the Shechemites for Shechem, who had fallen in love with their sister Dinah. Joseph's brothers were outraged, but then they made a deal with Shechem that they would be at peace with him and blend the families, *if* all of their men were circumcised. The men of Shechem agreed, but while they were still recovering, and in no position to fight, the sons of Jacob launched an assault on the city and destroyed it completely. When their father Jacob heard this, he was very angry and admonished his sons. (Refer to Genesis Chapter 34 Verses 30 for brief story.)

Another reason why Jacob liked Joseph more than his other sons was because Jacob really loved Rachel, Joseph's mother, and Joseph was the son of Jacob in his old age. (Refer to Genesis Chapter 37 Verse 3-10 for brief story.)

28) Answer: Joshua led the ancient Israelites into the Promise Land. (Refer to Joshua Chapter 1 Verse 9 for a brief story on how Joshua took over from Moses to lead the ancient Israelites into the Promise Land.)

29) Answer: Moses did not enter the Promise Land because he did not fully honour God in front of the ancient Israelites at the Waters of Meribah when he (Moses) struck the rock.

God then said to Moses and Aaron "because you did not trust me enough to demonstrate my holiness to the people of Israel, you will not lead them into the Land I am going to give them!" (Refer to Numbers Chapter 20 Verse 6-13, and Deuteronomy Chapter 32 Verse 48-52.)

30) Answer: Aaron, Moses' brother, died at Mountain Hor, the border of Edom. He was one hundred and twenty-three when he died. (Refer to Numbers Chapter 33 Verse 39, and Deuteronomy Chapter 10 Verse 6.)

31) Answer: Joseph's two sons in the Bible were Manasseh and Ephraim. According to the Bible, Manasseh means "God has made him (Joseph) forget all the troubles in his father's (Jacob) house." In the Bible, Ephraim means "God made me fruitful in this land of my grief."

32) Answer: Asenath was one of the Minor Biblical figures mentioned in the Old Testament Book of Genesis in the Bible. She is the wife of Joseph, one of the twelve sons of the Patriarch of ancient Israel. Asenath was the daughter of Potiphera. The Pharaoh gave Asenath as a wife to Joseph to marry. She was the daughter of Potiphera and gave birth to Manasseh and Ephrahim. (Refer to Genesis Chapter 41 Verse 45.)

33) Answer: Joseph was sold by his jealous half-brothers (except Reuben) to the Ishmaelite's for twenty pieces of silver who in turn took him to (ancient) Egypt and sold him to Potiphar, a captain of Pharaoh's bodyguard. (Refer to Genesis Chapter 39 Verse 1-16.)

111

34) Answer: According to Hebrew Ancestry, the names of the Patriarchs are: Abraham, Isaac, and Jacob. In the Bible, they play pivotal roles in the scriptures during and following their lifetime. (Refer to Genesis Chapter 17 Verse 7-8, Genesis Chapter 12 Verse 3, Genesis Chapter 22 Verse 18, Psalm 105 Verse 8-11, Galatians Chapter 3 Verse 26-29)

35) Answer: The Matriarchs, according to Hebrew Ancestry, are Sarah, Rebekah, Leah and Rachel. Some Jewish sources go further by including Bilhah and Zilpah. (Refer to Genesis Chapter 29 Verse 29, and Genesis Chapter 29 Verse 26)

36) Answer: The Five Books of Moses in the Book of the Old Testament of the Bible are:

• Genesis
• Exodus
• Leviticus
• Numbers
• Deuteronomy

37) Answer: Samson was the strongest ever character in the Bible. The source of his strength came from God. He was a Nazarite throughout his life. He was not meant to eat unclean food or cut his hair. He did, however, break his Nazarite vow. God used Samson mightily to deliver the ancient Israelites from the hands of their arch enemies such as the Philistines. He was one of the most popular judges in the Old Testament. He was a Judge over Israel for Twenty Years. (Refer to Judges Chapter 13, 14, 15, 16 Verse 1-31)

38) Answer: The role of the Judges in the Book of the Old Testament was to lead his people the ancient Israelites) between the conquest of the Promise Land (Canaan) and the

Unified Monarchy. During the period of The Judges, ancient Israel was renowned for drifting in and out of apostasy and when this happened God punished them by sending nations such as the Philistines, Moabites, Ammonites, and Amalekites to oppress them. When they cried and asked for forgiveness, God sent them Othniel, Ethud, Shamgar, Deborah, Gideon, Abimelech, Tola, Jair, Jephthah, Ibzan, Elon, Abdon, Samson, Eli, and Samuel. God worked miraculously and prophetically through the judges that ruled ancient Israel through the transition period.

39) Answer: Saul was the first King of the Unified Monarchy of Israel. He was from the tribe of Benjamin, one of the twelve tribes of ancient Israel. (Refer to 1 Samuel Chapter 9, and Chapter 10 to learn about King Saul)

40) Answer: Lot was Abraham's nephew in the Bible. Lot's wife turned into a pillar of salt as they were fleeing the destruction of Sodom and Gomorrah. Lot and his wife were warned by the Angels that God sent to rescue them to not look back; but she looked back and was turned into a pillar of salt. (Refer to Genesis Chapter 19 Verse 1-29 for story on Lot)

41) Answer: Moab and Ben-ammi were sons of Lot's two daughters who eventually went onto become the ancestors of the Moabites and Ammonites. (Refer to Genesis Chapter 19 Verse 30-36 for brief story)

42) Answer: Prophet Samuel's parents were Hannah and Elkanah. Elkanah lived in Ramah. He had two wives; Hannah and Peninnah. (Refer to 1 Samuel Chapter 1 1- 28)

43) Answer: Saul was rejected King of Israel because he refused to carry out God's instructions delivered through Prophet Samuel to utterly destroy the Amalekites. (Refer to 1 Samuel Chapter 15 Verse 10-30 to see brief story on Saul's rejection as King of Israel)

44) Answer: Eli was without doubt a godly Priest but did not reprimand his sons Hophini and Phinehas who had no regard or respect for God and his holy tabernacle. Eli knew what his sons were doing and refused to rein them in. His sons did not respect their duties as Priests in the tabernacle and treated God's offerings with contempt. It was the young Samuel who was being trained by Eli that prophesied many years later to Eli that he and his sons will be punished for his son's sinful behaviour, and that they will all die on the same day. (Refer to 1 Samuel Chapter 3 Verse 1-21, 1 Samuel Chapter 4 Verse 1-21 to learn more on how Eli and his family were punished.)

45) Answer: Phinehas' wife, on hearing the death of her husband, father-in-law, and capture of the Ark of God, gave birth to a boy she called "Ichabod" before she herself died. Ichabod means: "The glory had departed from Israel." (Refer to 1 Samuel Chapter 4 Verse 19)

46) Answer: Miriam and Aaron criticised Moses because he married a Cushite woman. Miriam felt Moses was getting all the attention. She had allowed some form of pride to set in. Miriam and Aaron felt that God should speak through them and not only Moses. God heard what Miriam and Aaron said and immediately summoned them out to the tabernacle. God punished Miriam by making her skin turn to leprosy. (Refer to Numbers Chapter 12 Verse 1-15 for full story)

47) Answer: Zipporah is mentioned in the Book of Exodus as the wife of Moses. She is one of the seven daughters of Jethro, the Prince of Midian. Jethro allowed Moses to marry Zipporah after saving his daughters and flock from competing herdsman. (Refer to Exodus Chapter 2 Verse 16-22 for brief story)

48) Answer: Gershom was the firstborn son of Moses and Zipporah. His name means 'sojourner in a foreign land'. (Refer to Exodus Chapter 2 Verse 21-22)

49) Answer: The Four Gospels in the book of the New Testament of the Bible are:

• Matthew
• Mark
• Luke
• John

50) Answer: Adam and Eve were driven out of the Garden of Eden because they disobeyed God's instruction of eating fruit from the Tree of Knowledge of Good and Evil. (Refer to Genesis Chapter 2 Verse 15-17)

51) Answer: Abraham's father in the Bible was Terah. Terah bore Abraham (Abram), Nahor, and Haran. (Refer to Genesis Chapter 11 Verse 27-32)

52) Answer: In the Bible, God said He would make Abraham's name great! Abram's name was changed to Abraham and Sarai, his wife, to Sarah. He (God) said he would bless those who bless Abraham, and that all the families of the earth would be blessed through Abraham. God fulfilled his promise by giving them a son called Isaac. Abraham the Patriarch became a father of many nations as

God promised in the Bible. (Refer to Genesis Chapter 12 Verse 1-3, Genesis Chapter 17 Verse 1-21)

53) Answer: Joshua was the leader after Moses that led the ancient Israelites into the Promise Land (Canaan) (Refer to Joshua Chapter 1 Verse 1-9)

54) Answer: Caleb is one of the individuals in the Old Testament that Moses sent out to spy on the ancient Land of Canaan. It was only Caleb and Joshua that came back giving a positive report. Caleb suggested that they (the ancient Israelites) should proceed immediately to take the land. In return, along with Joshua, God rewarded Caleb's faith with the promise that his descendants will enter and possess the Promise Land. (Refer to Numbers Chapter 13 and Chapter 14)

55) Answer: Joshua the son of Nun was also known as Hoshea. (Refer to Numbers Chapter 13 Verse 16)

56) Answer: The reason why Joshua and Caleb were of a different spirit was because they cultivated a "faith and winning mentality". They had seen all the amazing miracles that God had did by taking them (the ancient Israelites) out of ancient Egypt and through the Wilderness. Joshua and Caleb never complained and accepted Moses and Aaron as their leader. When Moses died, God saw Joshua was the perfect choice to lead the people into the Promise Land. They also believed in God's Commandments and Covenant and as a result received the promise of their descendants possessing the Promise Land.

57) Answer: Rahab was one of the female Minor Biblical Characters mentioned in the Old Testament. She hid two of the ancient Israelite spies that Joshua sent. The spies were sent to scout out the land on the ancient side of the River

Jordan and Jericho. The spies stayed at the house of Rahab, who was known as a "harlot".

After escaping, the spies promised to save Rahab and her family after taking the city of ancient Jericho. Rahab and her entire family were spared according to the promise of the spies and were incorporated among the ancient Jewish people.

Biblical interpreters have defined Rahab had a glaring example of faith, repentance, hospitality, and mercy in her interaction with Joshua's spies. (Refer to Joshua Chapter 2 Verse 1-24; Hebrews Chapter 11 Verse 31; James Chapter 2 Verse 25)

58) Answer: Eli was the Priest of Shiloh mentioned in The Old Testament. He had two sons called Hophini and Phinehas. He unknowingly accused Hannah (Elkanah's wife) of drunkenness when she came to the temple to pray for a child, but when she protested her innocence he wished her well. Hannah's eventual child, Samuel, was trained by Eli in the tabernacle. When Eli failed to admonish his sons for their sinful behaviour, God promised to punish his family, resulting immediately in the death of Eli and his sons on the same day. (Refer to 1 Samuel Chapter 1 Verse 1-18; 1 Samuel Chapter 2 Verse 12-16; 1 Samuel Chapter 4 Verse 11-22)

59) Answer: The two sons of Eli were Hophini and Phinehas.

60) Answer: Samuel's sons were Joel and Abijah. They did not follow in the upright and righteous path of their father. They were corrupt, took bribes, and perverted justice.

61) Answer: The reason why the ancient Israelites had requested for a king when Samuel grew old was because his two sons did not follow in the upright and righteous way as their father (Samuel), they had wanted to become like other

nations. They wanted a king! (Refer to 1 Samuel Chapter 8 Verse 1-22)

62) Answer: Samuel means "for I asked him of" or "enquired of him from the Lord". (Refer to 1 Samuel Chapter 1 Verse 19-20)

63) Answer: The Amalekites were one the ancient nations in the Bible that were enemies of the ancient nation of Israel. Amalek was the founder of the nation of the Amalekites and a grandson of Esau. The Amalekites were a recurrent foe and enemy of the ancient Israelites. (Refer to Exodus Chapter 17 Verse 8-16; 1 Samuel Chapter 30 Verse 1-2; 2 Samuel Chapter 1 Verse 5-10)

64) Answer: In the Bible, Jethro is mentioned in the Book of Exodus. He was Moses' father-in-law. He was a Kenite and the Priest in the land of Midian. He had seven daughters. His daughter Zipporah was Moses' wife. (Refer to Exodus Chapter 18 Verse 1-27)

65) Answer: Nine Female Characters that played a positive role in the Bible are:

• Sarah, the wife of Abraham, and who can be described as "The Mother of the Ancient Israelites or Jewish Nation" (Refer to Genesis Chapter 17 Verse 15-16). Despite God promising her a child, her impatience led her to influence Abraham to father a child with Hagar, Sarah's Egyptian handmaid; starting a conflict which continues to this day. Sarah does eventually give birth to Isaac, the child of promise just as God promised. Isaac goes on and becomes one of the Patriarchs of the nation of ancient Israel. We learn from Sarah that God's promise always comes to fruition.

• Rachel was one of Jacob's wives, only after Laban (Jacob's father-in-law) deceived Jacob in marrying Laban first. Jacob loved Rachel because she was prettier. (Refer to Genesis Chapter 29 Verse 1–29) Rachel and Leah carried on the tradition of Sarah giving their handmaids to Jacob. The four women gave birth to twelve boys and one girl. The sons went onto become heads of the twelve tribes of ancient Israel. Rachel's son Joseph had the most profound influence, saving ancient Israel during the famine in ancient Egypt. Rachel's younger son founded the Benjamin tribe and goes on to produce the first king of the Unified Monarch of Ancient Israel (King Saul) and one of the greatest Apostles in ancient times – The Apostle Paul.

• Leah was Jacob's first wife through a shameful trick hatched by Laban (his father-in-law). Maybe Jacob was getting a "taste of his own medicine" because this was similar to how he tricked his own father (Isaac) in getting his brother's (Esau) birth right. (Refer to Genesis Chapter 27 Verse 1-40). Jacob had worked hard for seven years to win Leah's younger sister Rachel. On the wedding night, her father Laban cleverly substituted Leah instead. Jacob discovered the deceit the following morning. With Jacob's true love for Rachel, he worked another seven years for Laban (his father-in-law) to eventually obtain Rachel as his wife. Leah went through a heart-breaking experience trying to win Jacob's love. The Bible shows how God graced and favoured Leah in a special way. Her son Judah, (which means "Praise") led the tribe that produced two of the most significant characters, Jesus Christ, Saviour of the world, and David who goes on to be ancient Israel's greatest ever king. Leah is truly a glaring example for individuals who try to earn God's love that is unconditional and there for those that need it.

• Jochebed was Moses' mother. She performed one of the most daring feats in history by giving up what she valued most by putting baby Moses in a waterproof basket and set it adrift on the Nile River. Pharaoh's daughter found and adopted the baby Moses as her own son. (Refer to Exodus Chapter 2 Verse 5-10) Even though Moses was raised as an Egyptian, he was chosen for a special assignment. God chose him to lead his people, the ancient Israelites, out of ancient Egypt. The faith of Jochebed saved Moses and propelled him to become Israel's greatest prophet and lawgiver.

• Miriam was Moses' elder sister. When her baby brother Moses floated down the River Nile in a basket to escape death from the ancient Egyptians, Miriam intervened with the Pharaoh's daughter offering Jochebed (Moses' real mother) as the baby's wet nurse. She played a significant role in the exodus of her people (the ancient Israelites) from Egypt. After the ancient Israelites crossed the Red Sea, Miriam was there leading the congregation in celebration (Refer to Exodus Chapter 15 Verse 20-22), her role as a Prophet led her to complain against Moses when he took a Cushite woman for a wife. God punished her for this insubordination. (Refer to Numbers Chapter 12 Verse 1-15)

• Rahab was one of the most peculiar characters in the Old Testament. In the Bible she is mentioned as a prostitute from Ancient Jericho. In exchange for hiding the Ancient Israel spies her whole family were saved when the ancient Israelites destroyed ancient Jericho. Rahab came to recognise the one and only true living God of Israel and was rewarded for it (Refer to Joshua Chapter 2 Verse 8-21; Joshua Chapter 6 Verse 22-25). Rahab's story can be likened to the people of ancient Nineveh also in the Old Testament. God sent the Prophet Noah to the people of Nineveh to turn from their wicked ways (Refer to Jonah Chapter 1, 2, 3, 4). Rahab did not have to continue in her sinful life after getting to know the true living God. God has no favourites. God is ready to embrace and show love, compassion, mercy, and grace to anyone who comes to believe in him. This is exactly what Rahab did and this is why her whole family were saved after the attack on ancient Jericho. She lived amongst the ancient

Israelites and was married to Salmon who was from the tribe of Judah. Rahab was also a relative of David (son of Jesse), the great king of ancient Israel.

- Deborah was one of the most influential characters during the era of the Judges in ancient Israel. Deborah was a Prophetess, Judge, and a brave warrior. She was the fourth Judge of Pre-Monarchic Israel and the only female judge named in the Bible. Her husband was Lapidoth. Deborah and Barak defeated Sisera. Deborah had instructed Barak to get ready because God was going to give victory to the ancient Israelites. (Refer to Judges Chapter 4 Verse 1-24) Deborah's faith in God and leadership skills caused her and Barak to be successful in defeating Sisera and the Canaanite army.

- Ruth was one of the most principled characters in the story of The Old Testament. She was a Moabite. Even though the story of Ruth is very few pages in the Bible, her character is so upright that it is a good model for Christians and Non-Christians to learn from. After her ancient Israelite mother-in-law (Naomi) decides to return to ancient Israel from the ancient land of Moab after the death of her husband and two sons, Ruth stays with Naomi despite Naomi bidding farewell to her daughters-in-law and encouraging them to stay with their people (the ancient Moabites). One of the daughter-in-law's (Orpah) kissed Naomi good-bye, but Ruth clung tightly to Naomi. Ruth replied: "Don't ask me to leave you and turn back. Wherever you go, I will go; wherever you live, I will live. Your people will be my people, and your God will be my God. Wherever you die, I will die, and there I will be buried. May God punish me severely if I allow anything but death to separate us" (Refer to Ruth Chapter 1, 2, 3). Ruth's character in the Bible is another example of God's mercy and love being extended to people outside of the ancient Jewish race. God wants every individual to come to the knowledge and understanding of his love, grace, and mercy.

- Esther is another character in The Book of the Old Testament in the Bible of prominence and reputable character. She was selected for a beauty contest to be the next Queen to the Persian King Xerxes. Harman, an ambitious and wicked official in the Quarters of the Persian King, callously devised a plan to have all the ancient Jews murdered because Mordecai (Esther's uncle) would not bow to him. Mordecai persuaded Esther (who had become the new Queen) to talk to the King to expose Haman's wicked plot and to reveal who she really was. Esther was able to gain the King's favour and Harman, along with all his family, were executed on the gallows that he had meant for Mordecai. Mordecai was promoted and the King passed a law for the Jews to unite and fight to defend themselves. The festival of Purim is a significant event in the Jewish calendar which commemorates the sparing of the Jewish People from Harman's plan of killing them as recounted in the Book of Esther in The Bible. What can be learnt from Esther's story is that we see that she stepped out in courage, proving God can save his people (all those who come to know, believe, and put their trust in him), even when the odds seem impossible.

66) Answer: Eliab, Abinadab, and Shimea are three of David's brothers. (Refer to 1 Samuel Chapter 16 Verse 8-13)

67) Answer: Jonathan was the eldest son of King Saul and a Prince of the Unified Kingdom of ancient Israel. He was also a close friend of David who eventually succeeded his father as King of Israel. Jonathan was one of most admired figures in the Old Testament and forged one of the best friendships with David (Refer to 1 Samuel Chapter 18 Verse 1-4). Jonathan and David's relationship was a platonic relationship. When David learns that his friend Jonathan is killed along with King Saul, his father, David composes one of the most moving poems he has ever written to honour Jonathan and

King Saul called the "Song of the Bow" (Refer to 2 Samuel Chapter 1 Verse 19-27). After Jonathan's death, and when David became king, he showed kindness to Jonathan's son Mehibosheth by allowing him to eat at the king's table. (Refer to 2 Samuel Chapter 9 Verse 1-12)

68) Answer: Saul was the first King of the Unified Kingdom of ancient Israel. He was anointed by the Prophet Samuel and was removed from office for failing to carry out God's instruction through Prophet Samuel to "completely destroy the Amalekites". (Refer to 1 Samuel Chapter 15 Verse 10-31)

69) Answer: Abner was a prominent secondary character in the Bible. He was the first Commander-in-Chief of the Unified Kingdom of ancient Israelite army. He was also King Saul's cousin. (Refer to 1 Samuel Chapter 14 Verse 50, Chapter 17 Verse 55; Chapter 26 Verse 5)

70) Answer: Ishbosheth was the fourth son of King Saul and the last remaining representative of his family to be king over the ancient Northern Kingdom of Israel after the death of his father and three brothers at the battle of Mount Gilboa. (Refer to 1 Samuel Chapter 31 Verse 1; 2 Samuel Chapter 2 Verse 10; 2 Samuel Chapter 2 Verse 4; 2 Samuel Chapter 2 Verse 12; 2 Samuel 3 Verse 1; 2 Samuel Chapter 3 Verse 6)

71) Answer: David was on the run from King Saul. David also had several opportunities to kill Saul but refused to do so. He said he would not put his hands on "God's anointed" while Saul was asleep. The Cave Adullam was the place that David used as a stronghold to seek refuge from King Saul. (Refer to 1 Samuel Chapter 22 Verse 1-2; 1 Samuel Chapter 24 Verse 1-22)

72) Answer: Ahithophel was one of King David's reliable and trusted advisers before turning traitor. He was renowned for his astute and wise counsel. During Prince Absalom's revolt against his father, King David, Ahithophel deserted David to support Absalom. (Refer to Psalm 3 Verse 1-8; 2 Samuel Chapter 15 Verse 12; 2 Samuel Chapter 15 Verse 31-37; 2 Samuel Chapter 16 Verse 15-23; 2 Samuel Chapter 17 Verse 1-14)

73) Answer: Hushai in the Bible was an Archite from the boarders of Ephraim. He was a friend of King David and acted as a spy during the rebellion of Absalom against David. Hushai was able to counter Ahithophel's advice and then send information to Zadok and Abiathar to warn David to flee before Absalom and his men attacked. (Refer to 2 Samuel Chapter 16 Verse 15-18; 2 Samuel Chapter 17 Verse 5-16)

74) Answer: Adonijah was the fourth son of King David. His mother's name was Haggith. Adonijah put himself forward as the apparent heir to succeed his father, King David. Although David, who was old, was aware of this and never rebuked or silenced Adonijah. David's silence could have been interpreted by Adonijah and others as consent. Adonijah consulted the support of Abiathar the High Priest and Joab, the Commander-in-Chief of the Unified ancient Israel army. (Refer to 1 King Chapter 1 Verse 1-6) After receiving news that Solomon was crowned king, Adonijah fled and took refuge at the altar. (Refer to 1 Kings Chapter 1 Verse 5-52; 1 Kings Chapter 2 Verse 13-25)

75) Answer: King Saul became jealous of David because he and all ancient Israel knew that he would one day succeed Saul as King. (Refer to 1 Samuel Chapter 18 Verse 1-16)

76) Answer: The reason why Joab was removed as Commander-in-Chief of the Unified Kingdom of Israel army was because he disobeyed King David's instructions of sparing his son, Prince Absalom's life. Although Joab was completely devoted to David, Joab felt that he had to act in the national interest of the kingdom by killing Absalom. Absalom had caused treason by trying to usurp his father from the throne. When he (Absalom) was discovered in an Oak Tree, he was immediately struck down by Joab (Refer to 2 Samuel Chapter 15 Verse 14; 2 Samuel Chapter 18 Verse 1-18). David was a broken man and grieved heavily for his son, Absalom. On hearing David's grief over Absalom, Joab confronted and admonished him. Although David followed Joab's advice to make a public appearance to thank and encourage his soldiers (Refer to 2 Samuel Chapter 19 Verse 1-8; 2 Samuel Chapter 19 Verse 13-14), deep down in his heart David never forgot or forgave Joab for killing Absalom. However, David could not exert revenge immediately on Joab because he (Joab) had become powerfully and influentially strong and maybe because David did not want to start a war with his Commander-in-Chief which could cause an internal conflict. It was on the brink of death that David probably was able to have Absalom's death avenged by asking Solomon to have Joab killed, "cleverly citing" the deaths of Abner the son of Ner and Amasa the son of Jether for having Joab executed. (Refer to 1 Kings Chapter 2 Verse 28-34)

77) Answer: David reigned for forty years over the Unified Kingdom of ancient Israel. He was 33 years when he ascended the throne. He first reigned over Judah for seven years and then Israel and Judah for 33 years. He reigned in the highest and most prosperous period of ancient Israel's era, called by the "Golden Age". David is depicted in The Old and New Testament as model king of piety, repentance, and submission. (Refer to 1 Kings Chapter 11 Verse 36-39)

78) Answer: Sheba, the son of Bichri, was from the tribe of King Saul; an ancient Benjamite. After David returned to Jerusalem after defeating Absalom, another strife broke out. There was a strife between Israel (the ten Northern ancient tribes) and Judah because Judah took the lead in welcoming back King David. Sheba took advantage of this by stirring up more trouble, saying: "What inheritance or interest do we have in the son of Jesse." All the people of ancient Israel followed Sheba and deserted David, leaving just the people of ancient Judah loyal to David. David then instructed Amasa (his other nephew) who he had made Commander-in-Chief in place of Joab to assemble the army of ancient Judah in three days and report back. For some reason, Amasa was delayed longer than the set time that David had appointed to him; David therefore turned to Abishai, another one of his nephew's (Joab's elder brother) and said: "Sheba could do more damage to us than Absalom, take my men and go after Sheba before he finds refuge in a fortified city and we are unable to catch him." This operation provided the opportunity for Joab to win his job back as Commander-in-Chief of the ancient army. He eliminated Amasa (who David had made Commander-in-Chief of the ancient army in his place), restored order to the army and pursued after Sheba with his brother Abishai. Joab pursued Sheba to Abel-beth-maachah and threatened to destroy the city if Sheba was not given up. An unnamed wise woman of the city negotiated with Joab. Sheba was killed by the city and his head was thrown down from the city tower wall to Joab. Joab then blew his trumpet and ordered his troops to return to David in ancient Jerusalem. Joab saved the day by repelling the revolt against David. Joab returned to David in ancient Jerusalem and was Commander-in-Chief of the army once again. (Refer to 2 Samuel Chapter 20 Verse 4-23)

79) Answer: David put a stone in his sling from some smooth stones chosen from the brook; hurled it in the air and hit the

giant Philistine in the forehead. Goliath fell back and hit the ground. David ran and stood over to the Philistine drew his sword out of the sheath and killed him, then cut his head off with it. (Refer to 1 Samuel Chapter 17 Verse 40, 49-51)

80) Answer: Ahimelech was the twelfth High Priest of ancient Israel. He officiated at ancient Nob (an ancient place in Israel, also near to ancient Jerusalem) He was the son of Ahitub and father of Abiathar. Ahimelech also comes from the family line of Aaron's son Ithamar, and from the line of Eli, a former priest of ancient Israel. David, while on the run from King Saul, came to Ahimelech for help.

Ahimelech gave David and his companion five loaves of Show bread or Shew bread (Holy bread dedicated to God) and a sword. He was summoned into King Saul's presence and was accused of disloyalty for helping David on the information given by Doeg the Edomite. Saul ordered Doeg the Edomite to kill Ahimelech and all his family household. Doeg did as Saul instructed and killed eighty-five individuals who wore a linen ephod. Saul also struck the City of Nob, killing infants, children, men, women, and cattle. One of Ahimelech's sons – Abiathar – managed to escape and tell David that Saul had killed all God's priests in Nob. (Refer to 1 Samuel Chapter 21 Verse 1-9; 1 Samuel Chapter 22 Verse 8-23)

81) Answer: God was very angry with King Solomon because when he was told his (Solomon's) heart was not loyal to God like his father David was. God almighty had appeared to Solomon twice, warning him specifically about worshipping other gods, but Solomon ignored God's command. Solomon was going to pay dearly for his apostasy by having the Kingdom of the Unified Kingdom of ancient Israel torn away from him, but God was going to defer the punishment for the sake of his father King David who had walked upright

before God, and for the sake of ancient Jerusalem which God had chosen. The punishment happened during the reign of Rehoboam, his son. (Refer to 1 Kings Chapter 11 Verse 1-13)

82) Answer: David and six hundred loyal people (including his household) fled to the land of the Philistines from King Saul. He was there until the death of King Saul. Achish, the son of Maoch, King of Gath, entertained David and his companions. He was given the land of Ziklag. Ziklag has belonged to Israel to this very day. While David was in Ziklag he raided the Geshurites, Girzites, and the Amalekites. David stayed in the land of Gath for one year and six months.

83) Answer: When the Queen of Sheba heard of all the fame and wisdom of Solomon, she came to visit him and test him with difficult questions. She came to ancient Jerusalem with a great entourage, and with camels that bore spices, gold, and precious stones. The Bible narrates that she was very impressed, speechless with what she saw. She also gave praise to God for setting Solomon on the throne of ancient Israel. She gave King Solomon one hundred and twenty talents of gold and spices in great quantity. Solomon gave all that the Queen of Sheba desired, whatever she asked, besides what Solomon gave her according to royal generosity. (Refer to 1 Kings Chapter 10 Verse 1-13)

84) Answer: The Unified Kingdom of ancient Israel was split because of King Solomon's disobedience of worshipping false gods and idols. Solomon was warned by God of the consequences of his apostasy. The Kingdom was going to be torn away from him – Solomon. (Refer to 1 Kings Chapter 11 Verse 11-13)

85) Answer: Joab was the person that led the assault on the Jebusites and helped take the ancient city for David; thus becoming the ancient City of King David.

Joab was the son of Zeruiah, and the nephew of King David. He went on to do many great deeds on the military field for David. (Refer to 2 Samuel Chapter 8 Verse 16; 2 Samuel Chapter 20 Verse 23; 1 Chronicles Chapter 11 Verse 6, 8; 1 Chronicles Chapter 18 Verse 15; 1 Chronicles Chapter 27 Verse 34)

86) Answer: Benaiah. Benaiah was the son of Jehoiada. He was named as one of King David's mighty men. The Bible recounts how he killed two lion-like Moabite Soldiers, killed a lion in the midst of a pit on a snowy day (Refer to 2 Samuel Chapter 23 Verse 20-23) He was also in charge of the Cherethites and the Pelethites. David also appointed him over his guard.

87) Answer: Jabez was a minor character in the Old Testament. He was from the family of Judah. The Bible narrates that he was more honourable than his brothers. His mother called him "Jabez" meaning that he was born in pain. The Bible also states that Jabez called on God asking to be blessed, his quarters enlarged, asking for God to be with him, to be kept from evil, and that he does not cause pain. Jabez prayer to God can be likened to King Solomon's prayer when he (Solomon) asked God for wisdom to rule ancient Israel. (Refer to 1 Chronicles Chapter 3 Verse 9-11; 1 Kings Chapter 3 Verse 6-13)

88) Answer: Lot is mentioned as Abraham's nephew in the Old Testament. Lot was born in Ur, the Chaldeans. He travelled with Abraham until they split company. He was saved from the destruction of Sodom and Gomorrah, during which

his wife become a pillar of salt. Lot and his daughters escaped to Zoar. (Refer to Genesis Chapter 12 Verse 4; Genesis Chapter 13 Verse 7-13; Genesis Chapter 19 Verse 1-38)

89) Answer: Lot's wife turned into a pillar of salt. She was told by God's Angels who had come to rescue them (Lot, his wife, and two daughters) not to look back when Sodom and Gomorrah were being destroyed, but she disobeyed and looked back; hence turning into a pillar of salt. (Refer to Genesis Chapter 19 Verse 24-26)

90) Answer: According to the Biblical narrative, Moab and Ammon were born to Lot and Lot's elder daughter and younger daughter in the aftermath of the destruction of Sodom and Gomorrah. (Refer to Genesis Chapter 19 Verse 37-38)

91) Answer: Asahel was the younger brother of Abishai and Joab, and nephew of King David. He was killed by Abner whom he was pursuing from a battlefield when fighting against him in Gibeon. He was known for his swiftness of foot, like a wild deer. (Refer to 2 Samuel Chapter 2 Verse 18-23) He was also mentioned amongst David's valiant men. (Refer to 2 Samuel Chapter 23 Verse 24)

92) Answer: Solomon asked God for wisdom; to have an understanding heart to judge his people; to be able to discern between good and evil. The Bible states that this request pleased God. (Refer to I Kings Chapter 3 Verse 9-10)

93) Answer: The ancient Israelites were in ancient Egypt for four hundred and thirty years. (Refer to Exodus Chapter 12 Verse 41)

94) Answer: Delilah and Jezebel are two characters in the bible that were manipulative in achieving their aims. (Refer to Judges Chapter 16 Verse 1-22; 1 Kings Chapter 19 Verse 1; 1 Kings Chapter 21 Verse 5-16)

95) Answer: Jehoshaphat was the fourth King of the ancient Judah. He was the son of Asa, and his mother's name was Azubah. He was commended for suppressing of idolatrous worship of "High Places" (False gods). (Refer to 2 Chronicles Chapter 17 Verse 6) God also gave Jehoshaphat victory of the Moabites and Ammonites (Refer to 2 Chronicles Chapter 20 Verse 1-30)

96) Answer: Ahab was the seventh King of the ancient Kingdom of Israel and the husband of Jezebel. In the Bible, Ahab was described as a wicked King, particularly for condoning Jezebel's influence on idol religious practices, and his key role in ordering the arbitrary execution of Naboth. (Refer to 1 Kings Chapter 19 Verse 1; 1 Kings Chapter 21 Verse 5-29; 1 Kings Chapter 22 Verse 29-40)

97) Answer: Elijah was one of the Major Prophets in the Books of the Old Testament. He was one of the most influential Prophets in ancient Israel. He challenged the ancient Israelites to stop "faltering" and serve God wholeheartedly or serve Baal. After he defended the worship of Almighty God, Yahweh, he seized all four hundred and fifty false prophets of Baal and had them all executed. (Refer to 1 Kings Chapter 18 Verse 20-41) Elijah revived the son of the widow from Zarephath. (Refer to 1 Kings Chapter 17 Verse 17-24). He also denounced King Ahab for his crimes and reminding him that everyone was subject to the law of God, Almighty. (Refer to 1 Kings Chapter 21 Verse 17-21) Elijah is taken up to heaven in a whirlwind. (Refer to 2 Kings Chapter 2 Verse 1-14)

98) Answer: Judas Iscariot was a disciple and one of the original disciples of Jesus Christ. All four Gospel in the New Testament of the Bible mentions how he betrays Jesus Christ to the Sanhedrin in the Garden of Gethsemane by kissing Jesus Christ and addressing him as "RABBI" to reveal his identity to the Roman soldiers that were coming to arrest him. (Refer to Matthew Chapter 26 Verse 36-56; Mark Chapter 14 Verse 32-50; Luke Chapter 22 Verse 40-53; John Chapter 18 Verse 1-11)

99) Answer: King Ahab of ancient Israel had Naboth executed for his Vineyard. (Refer to 1 Kings Chapter 21 Verse 2-16)

100) Answer: Jezebel in The Old Testament Book of the Bible was probably the most deceitful and evil character ever. Delilah, another deceitful character mentioned in the Book of Judges (Refer to Judges Chapter 16 Verse 1-20), doesn't even come close to her; Jezebel makes her (Delilah) look ordinary. Ahab who married her (Jezebel) should have learnt from the mistake of one of his earlier predecessors (King Solomon) who went down the road of idolatry (Refer to 1 Kings Chapter 11 Verse 1-11). Jezebel the daughter of the Priest-King of Ethbaal, ruler of the Cities of Tyre and Sidon took Ahab, The King of ancient Israel down the route of Baal worship. (Refer to 1 Kings Chapter 18 Verse 17-40)

101) Answer: Jehu was anointed by Prophet Elijah (Refer to 1 Kings Chapter 19 Verse 16). His assignment was to eliminate the descendants of Ahab and Jezebel along with the priests of the god of Baal (Refer to 2 Chronicles Chapter 22 Verse 7; 2 King Chapter 9 Verse 30-37)

102) Answer: Mordecai was one of the main personalities in the Book of Esther. He adopted his orphan cousin Hadassah (Esther) whom he looked after as his own daughter (Refer to Esther Chapter 2 Verse 7). Mordecai sat within the King's gate and overhead a conversation plot to kill King Ahasuerus. He revealed the matter to Esther who then informed the King in Mordecai's name. (Refer to Esther Chapter 2 Verse 19-23)

Mordecai was promoted by King Ahasuerus to Haman's position after Haman's conspiracy to eliminate all the ancient Jews in ancient Persia. (Refer to Esther Chapter 3 Verse 1-15; Esther Chapter 4, Chapter 5, Chapter 6, and Chapter 7)

103) Answer: The antagonist was in the book of Esther was Haman. Haman was a cruel general that worked for King Ashasuerus who made a treacherous decree for Mordecai and the ancient Jews in ancient Persia to be destroyed all because Mordecai would not bow to him. Haman went to the extent of setting up gallows for Mordecai to hang on. When Esther revealed Haman's evil plan of trying to execute the ancient Jews to King Ashasuerus, the King had Haman and all his family hanged on the gallows instead. (Refer to Esther Chapter 5, 7, 8, 9, and 10)

104) Answer: In the Bible, Solomon's other name was Jedidiah. This was the blessing name given by God through the instruction of Prophet Nathan to the baby Solomon, the second child of King David and Bathsheba. Jedidiah means "because of God." (Refer to 2 Samuel Chapter 12 Verse 24-25)

105) Answer: Hosea, Joel, Amos, Obadiah, Jonah, Micah, Nahum, Habakkuk, Zephaniah, Haggai, Zechariah, and Malachi are the twelve 'Minor Prophets' in the Old

Testament. Although they were known as Minor Prophets these Prophets were used by God to deliver important prophetic messages to the ancient Israelites before the fall of the ancient Northern Kingdom (Israel), and Southern Kingdom (Judah), and after return from exile.

106) Answer Rehoboam was the son of Solomon and Naamah. He succeeded his father King Solomon as the next king. As God prophesied before Solomon died, the ten Northern tribes of ancient Israel split and was ruled by Jeroboam while he (Rehoboam) ruled the ancient Southern tribes of Israel. (Refer to 1 Kings Chapter 12 Verse 1-24)

107) Answer: Jeroboam (the first) was the first king of the ancient Split Northern Kingdom of Israel. His father's name was Nebat and mother's name was Zeruah. During Solomon's reign when he (Solomon) saw that Jeroboam was industrious he put him in charge of the labour force of the House of Joseph. When Jeroboam went out of ancient Jerusalem, he encountered Prophet Ahijah, a Levite Prophet during the reign of Solomon , who foretold to Jeroboam that he would one day become king and that God was going to chastise The House of David because of Solomon's apostasy. When Solomon heard this, he tried to kill Jeroboam who then fled to ancient Egypt until Solomon's death. (Refer to 1 Kings Chapter 11 Verse 26-40)

When Jeroboam became king of the ancient Northern Kingdom of Israel he feared that the people would go back to the House of David (ancient Southern Kingdom of Israel) and therefore introduced pagan worship to ancient Northern Kingdom of Israel. (Refer to 1 Kings Chapter 12 Verse 25 – 33) With Jeroboam, doing the same as Solomon by breaking the mandate of the Torah of worshipping false gods, God severely punished the House of Jeroboam. (Refer to 1 Kings Chapter 14 Verse 1-20)

108) Answer: Naamah was the mother of Rehoboam. She was an Ammonitess and one of the seven hundred wives and concubines of Solomon; one of the foreign wives he married. (Refer to 1 Kings Chapter 14 Verse 31; 2 Chronicles Chapter 12 Verse 13)

109) Answer: Abijah was the second king of the ancient Southern Kingdom of Israel. He was the son of Rehoboam. His mother's name was Maachah. There was constant war between the ancient Northern Kingdom of Israel and ancient Southern Kingdom of Israel under Abijah. (Refer to 2 Chronicles Chapter 13 Verse 1-22) The Bible states that Abijah walked in total disobedience like his father Rehoboam. (Refer to 1 Kings Chapter 15 Verse 1-8)

110) Answer: There are four Major Prophets in the Old Testament Book of the Bible. They are:

• Isaiah
• Jeremiah
• Ezekiel
• Daniel

111) Answer: God instructed Prophet Elijah to go to ancient Zarephath because he had made supernatural provision for Prophet Elijah to be fed by a widow. (Refer to 1 Kings Chapter 17 Verse 8-16) Another reason why God had instructed Elijah to go ancient Zarephath was that God was going to perform something in the life of the Zarephath widow that was going to change her faith and belief. (Refer to 1 Kings Chapter 17 Verse 17-24)

112) Answer: Two characters in the Bible gifted by God that had the knowledge and ability to interpret dreams were

Joseph (Refer to Genesis Chapter 40 Verse 1-23; Genesis Chapter 41 Verse 1 – 39) and Daniel. (Refer to Daniel Chapter 2 Verse 1-48; Daniel Chapter 5 Verse 11-29)

113) Answer: The Book of Lamentations in the Bible is a combination of poetic lament descriptions of the fall and destruction of ancient Jerusalem. It proceeds the Book of Jeremiah in the Old Testament. Jeremiah is the author of the Book of Lamentations. The Book of Lamentations is one of the shortest Books in the Bible. (Refer to Lamentations Chapter 1, 2, 3, 4, and 5)

114) Answer: Jonah, the son of Amittai, was one of the Minor Prophets in the Bible. According to the narrative in the Bible, he was sent by God to the ancient City of Nineveh to preach repentance and salvation to the people of Nineveh. He disobeys God and flees to Tarshish on a ship. God then sends a great storm on the sea so that the ship was about to be broken up. The sailors were terrified and every person on board cried out to their god, but Jonah had gone to the lower deck and was fast asleep. The captain of the ship approached him and asked why he was sleeping and that he (Jonah) should call on God so they do not perish. The sailors decided to cast lots and they found out that Jonah was the cause of the trouble. Jonah then told them to throw him into the sea and the sea stopped raging. God then prepared a great fish to swallow him up. (Refer to Jonah Chapter 1 Verse 1-17)

115) Answer: The people of ancient Nineveh were a foreign nation outside of the ancient Jewish or Hebrew nation. The ancient Ninevites, according to the narrative in the Bible, were a wicked sinful nation. God wanted them to hear the preaching of Jonah so that they could turn from their wicked sinful way. The preaching was a success and God showed compassion and mercy to the Ninevites. (Refer to Jonah

Chapter 3 Verse 10)

116) Answer: Hananiah (Shadrach), Mishael (Meshach), Azariah (Abed-nego) Note: That the names in brackets denote their Babylonian names. They were Daniel's (Belteshazzar) friends and they all came from the tribe of Judah.(Refer to Daniel Chapter 1 Verse 6-7)

117) Answer: In the Bible, the Hebrew name Daniel means "God Is My Judge." Daniel is also one of the Major Prophets in the Old Testament of the Hebrew Bible.

118) Answer: Nebuchadnezzar II was one of the most powerful kings in ancient Mesopotamia. In addition to Nebuchadnezzar restoring the Neo-Babylonian Empire to its former glory, he was known in the Bible in 589 BC to have invaded and destroyed Jerusalem and the First Temple and took a lot of inhabitants of Judah into the Neo-Babylonian Empire where they were taught the literature and language of the Chaldeans. Among the people from Judah were Daniel, Shadrach, Meshach, and Abed-Nego (Refer to Daniel Chapter 1 Verse 1-7). Nebuchadnezzar was also known in the Bible to have constructed a gold image statue and ordered everyone to bow to this image, but Shadrach, Meshach, and Abed-Nego refused to bow to the gold image statue, when Nebuchadnezzar heard that they had refused he told them that they would be immediately cast into the burning fiery furnace. They told the King that the true living God that they had put their trust in would deliver them from the burning fiery furnace. (Refer to Daniel Chapter 3 Verse 1-30)

Nebuchadnezzar, also during the peak of his reign, allowed pride to get in the way, but God, Almighty humbled him. Nebuchadnezzar without a doubt was the absolute ruler in ancient Mesopotamia, but he came to swiftly realise that it was God, Almighty and not he (Nebuchadnezzar) that was in control, and that all kings, queens, or rulers of any kind are subject or accountable to God's directions. (Refer to Daniel Chapter 2 Verse 21; Daniel Chapter 4 Verse 17; Daniel Chapter 4 Verse 28-33; Daniel Chapter 4 Verse 34-37)

119) Answer: The Neo-Assyrian Empire flourished between 911 and 609 BC. It was an Iron Age Mesopotamian Empire. The Neo-Assyrian Kingdom had five capitals. They were Assur (911 BC), Nimrud (879 BC), Khorsabad (706 BC), Nineveh (705 BC), and Harran (612 BC) The Assyrian Capital of Nineveh fell in 612 (BC) after three months of war. The Neo-Assyrian Empire (Nineveh) had the opportunity of knowing the true God. Under Jonah's preaching Nineveh had turned from their sinful ways and God graciously stayed his judgement, but a hundred years later the prophet Nahum foretold the decline of the City of Nineveh because they had forgotten their revival and returned to their old ways of violence, adultery, and arrogance. As a result, Babylon destroyed the City of Nineveh. (Refer to Jonah Chapter 1 Verse 1-2; Jonah Chapter 3 Verse 1-10; Nahum Chapter 1, 2, and 3)

120) Answer: According to the Biblical narrative, Belshazaar holds a feast (Refer to Daniel Chapter 5 Verse 1-30) and drinks from the vessels that had been looted from the First Temple (of God) in Jerusalem. A hand appears and writes on the wall. Belshazaar becomes terrified. Like his father (Nebuchadnezzar) had done, he called his magicians, but they were not able to interpret the writing. Daniel was eventually called and reminded Belshazaar that he would face the same fate as his father because he (Belshazzar) had not recognised that it was God Almighty that had supremacy over kingdoms.

God had finally numbered Belshazaar's days; he had been weighed, and found wanting, and his kingdom was given to the Medes and Persians (the ancient Iranians) (Refer to Daniel Chapter 5 Verse 30-31)

121) Answer: Elizabeth and Zechariah were the parents of John the Baptist. Briefly, according to the Biblical narrative, Zachariah was standing by the right altar when he (Zachariah) saw an Angel (Gabriel). e was startled and gripped with fear. The Angel assured him and told him not to be afraid and told him that their prayers had been heard, that they will have a child and the name of the child will be called John. (Refer to Luke Chapter 1 Verse 5-22)

122) Answer: John the Baptist was the son of Elizabeth and Zachariah. He had a very important mission. He was the forerunner of Our Lord and Saviour (of the world) Jesus Christ. John the Baptist was an ancient Jewish itinerant preacher. According to the narrative in the Book of the New Testament of the Bible, John the Baptist went into all the regions around ancient Jordan preaching baptism and repentance for the remission of sins. Just as it was written in the book of Isaiah in the Bible, "The voice of one crying in the wilderness: prepare the way of the Lord; make his paths straight. Every valley shall be filed, and every mountain and hill brought low; the crocked places shall be made straight, and the rough ways smooth, and all flesh shall see the salvation of God." The above quotation was used to signify that John the Baptist was preparing the way for Jesus Christ as foretold by the Prophet Isaiah. (Refer to Isaiah Chapter 40 Verse 3-5; Luke Chapter 3 Verse 1-6)

John the Baptist was imprisoned for speaking out against Herod Antipas for divorcing his wife and unlawfully taking Herodias, the wife of his brother Herod Philip I. On Antipas' (Herod) birthday, Salome, Herodias' daughter, danced before Antipas who was very impressed that he promised to give her anything she desired. To get revenge for criticising her marriage (to Antipas) Herodias told Salome to ask for the head of John the Baptist on a platter. Although Antipas was dismayed by the request, he reluctantly ordered John the Baptist to be executed in prison in Machaerus, Jordan. (Refer to Matthew Chapter 14 Verse 1-12; Mark Chapter 6 Verse 14-29)

123) Answer: Zedekiah was the twentieth and last king of ancient Judah (from the House of David), before it was destroyed by ancient Babylon. He was installed as King of ancient Judah by Nebuchadnezzar II, King of Babylon, after a siege of ancient Jerusalem in 597 BC to succeed his nephew Jeconiah who was deposed as king after a reign of three months and ten days.

According to the Biblical narrative, Zedekiah (or Mattaniah) did evil in the sight of God just like Jehoiakim and Jehoiachin before him (Refer to 2 King Chapter 24 Verse 17-20). God was so angry with the ancient people of Judah that he finally cast them out of his presence and gave them into the hands of ancient Babylon or the Neo-Babylonian Empire who had been the new military power in Mesopotamia. Zedekiah refused to heed the counsel of Prophet Jeremiah during his reign (Refer to 2 Kings Chapter 24 Verse 19-20; Jeremiah Chapter 52 Verse 2-3).

At the end of Zedekiah's eleven-year reign (of ancient Judah), Nebuchadnezzar II succeeded in capturing ancient Judah. Zedekiah and his entourage tried to escape the city but were captured by Nebuchadnezzar II forces. Zedekiah's sons were put to death in his presence. Zedekiah had his eyes plucked by the ancient Babylonian forces and was placed in prison till his death. (Refer to Jeremiah Chapter 52 Verse 1-11; 2 Kings Chapter 24 Verse 17-20; Jeremiah Chapter 25 Verse 1-8)

124) Answer: Gerhazi in the Bible was the assistant to Prophet Elisha. He was in a unique position but was fundamentally

dishonest, abusing his position to cheat Naaman, the Syrian general afflicted with leprosy. Elisha castigated his conduct with righteous sternness and pronounced that the leprosy on Naaman would cleave to him (Gerhazi) and his descendants forever (Refer to 2 King Chapter 5 Verse 21-27). Gerhazi also appears in the story of the Shunammite woman (Refer to 2 Kings Chapter 4 Verse 12-16).

125) Answer: The Shunammite woman is a minor character in the Book of the Old Testament during the time of Prophet Elisha. The Bible describes her as a "notable woman" (See KJV) (Refer to 2 Kings Chapter 4 Verse 8-10).

126) Answer: The First Temple is the other name that Solomon's Temple was known as. According to the Biblical narrative, King Solomon, David's son, was the person that constructed the First Temple. Solomon was the last King of the Unified Kingdom of ancient Israel and Judah, and during the time of ancient Kingdom of Judah the temple was dedicated to God. (Refer to I Kings Chapter 8 Verse 62-66; I Kings Chapter 9 Verse 1-9)

The First Temple stood from 1000 to 586 BC before its destruction by Nebuchadnezzar II after the siege of ancient Jerusalem in 587 BC.

127) Answer: Naaman, according to the Biblical narrative in the Old Testament, was the Commander of the ancient Syrian army. He had leprosy and was eventually healed by God following the instructions of Prophet Elisha who told Naaman to dip himself seven times in the River Jordan (Refer to II Kings Chapter 5 Verse 8-16).

128) Answer: According to the Bible, John the Baptist ate locust and wild honey. (Refer to Matthew Chapter 3 Verse 4)

129) Answer: Jonah spent three days and three nights in the belly of the whale. (Refer to Jonah Chapter 1 Verse 17)

130) Answer: In the Bible, John the Baptist was described as "The Forerunner" of our Lord and Saviour Jesus Christ. John the Baptist, as the New Testament Gospel describes, was the one that prepared the way. He was "The voice of one crying in the wilderness." He was calling people to repentance. (Refer to Matthew Chapter 3 Verse 1-9)

131) Answer: The Book of Matthew in the New Testament was written by Matthew who was an Evangelist and one of the original twelve disciples of Jesus Christ.

He was a Jewish Christian writing to his countrymen. The Jewish Community was led by the Pharisees and Rabbis who had assumed control of the ancient Jewish people in the aftermath of the destruction of Jerusalem by Nebuchadnezzar. The Book of Matthew, out of the three Synoptic Gospels, is the only Book that traces the genealogy of Jesus Christ. Matthew's aim was to show that Jesus Christ was The King of the Jews, the anticipated Messiah.

Matthew, through a painstakingly series of Old Testament quotations, is able to document Jesus Christ's claim as the Messiah. His (Jesus Christ's) genealogy, baptism, messages, and miracles all point to the same inevitable inference.

Historians suggest that Matthew wrote his Gospel between 80 CE and 90 CE.

132) Answer: In the Old Testament Bible, Moses was described as the Law Giver. God chose Moses to lead the ancient Israelites out of ancient Egypt to the edge of the ancient Promise Land and to meditate his covenant with them. (Refer to Exodus Chapter 20 Verse 1-17)

133) Answer: The Gospel of Matthew was writing about the Jewish Messiah, Jesus Christ. Matthew, the author of the Gospel, was writing to his fellow countrymen.

134) Answer: Satan tempted Jesus Christ in the wilderness. (Refer to Matthew Chapter 4 Verse 1-11)

135) Answer: on the Sea of Galilee, Jesus called Simon, known as Peter, and Andrew his brother. Later he saw James and John who were also brothers. James and John left their father, Zebedee. (Refer to Matthew Chapter 4 Verse 18)

136) Answer: There are twenty-seven books in the New Testament part of the Bible:

- Matthew
- Mark
- Luke
- John
- Acts of Apostles
- Romans
- I Corinthians
- II Corinthians
- I Thessalonians
- II Thessalonians
- I Timothy
- II Timothy
- Titus
- Philemon
- Hebrews
- James
- I Peter
- II Peter

- I John
- II John
- III John
- Jude
- Revelation

137) Answer: Luke was the writer of the Book of Luke as well as the Acts of the Apostle which would mean that he would have contributed a quarter of the text of the New Testament. He was a Physician by profession. He is mentioned in the New Testament a couple of times as a Physician and a Disciple of Apostle Paul. (Refer Colossians Chapter 4 Verse 14; Philemon Chapter 1 Verse 24; 2 Timothy Chapter 4 Verse 11)

138) Answer: Apostle Paul wrote thirteen Books of the New Testament Bible.

They are:

- Romans
- I Corinthians
- II Corinthians
- Galatians
- Ephesians
- Philippians
- Colossians
- I Thessalonians
- II Thessalonians
- I Timothy
- II Timothy
- Titus
- Philemon

139) Answer: Saul of ancient Tarsus (Turkey) who later became Apostle Paul on his conversion was the person that persecuted the early Church in the First Century World in the Book of Acts of the Apostles in the Bible. (Refer to Acts Chapter 9 Verse 13-16)

140) Answer: Apostle Peter was the Disciple that denied knowing Jesus Christ in the Bible when the rooster crowed three times. (Refer to Matthew Chapter 26 Verse 33-35)

141) Answer: Apostle Peter, who was one of the original twelve disciples of Jesus Christ in the Bible, is widely believed to have written I Peter and II Peter. The Apostle Peter was writing to the ancient Jewish Christians as well as the ancient people in Anatolia, Asia Minor, Turkey, and to the various churches in Asia Minor. (Refer to I Peter and II Peter)

142) Answer: Stephen was a Greek-speaking Hellenist selected by the original twelve disciples to participate in a fairer distribution to the Greek-speaking Hellenist widows. He was a Christian Deacon in Jerusalem and the first Christian Martyr in the first century of the early church to be killed in the defence of his faith (preaching the Gospel of Jesus Christ) before the Rabbinic Court. His address to the Diaspora Jews offended them and he was charged for blasphemy. His death was witnessed by Saul of Tarsus, a Pharisee who later become a follower of Jesus Christ. (Refer to Acts Chapter 7)

143) Answer: Peter one of the original twelve disciples mentioned in the Bible tried to walk on water before he started to sink. (Refer to Matthew Chapter 14 Verse 28-33)

144) Answer: Apostle Andrew was among the original twelve disciples called by Jesus Christ. He was also the brother of Simon Peter. He was a fisherman by profession. In the Gospels of Matthew and Mark it is recorded that both disciples were called together to become disciples of Jesus Christ. (Refer to Matthew Chapter 4 Verse 18-22; Mark Chapter 1 Verse 16-20)

145) Answer: Ananias and Sapphira were members of the Early Church in the Book of Acts in the Bible. Ananias and Sapphira died after lying to the Holy Spirit. (Refer to Acts of Apostles Chapter 5 Verse 1-10)

146) Answer: Angel Gabriel was God's key arch angel mentioned in the Bible. Angel Gabriel was sent by God to give Daniel the interpretation of two important dreams he (Daniel) was trying to find the answer to. (Refer to Daniel Chapter 8 Verse 15-26; Daniel Chapter 9 Verse 21-27)

Angel Gabriel was also the Angel that God used to visit Zachariah and for the Annunciation of the Virgin Mary to respectively foretell the birth of John the Baptist and Jesus Christ. (Refer to Luke Chapter 1 Verse 11-38)

147) Answer: The ancient Christian believers that gathered together in an upper room in Jerusalem were all in one accord as the Bible describes and the Holy Spirit fell on them like tongues of fire. (Refer to Acts of Apostles Chapter 2 Verse 1-13) The Christian Day of Pentecost is a Christian Holy Day. It is usually marked five days after Easter Sunday which commemorates the descent of the Holy Spirit upon the Apostles and other followers of Jesus Christ while they were in Jerusalem. It is also known as "WhitSunday" which is used in Britain, Ireland, and throughout the world amongst Christian denominations such as: Protestant, Catholic,

Anglican, and Methodist that celebrate this Christian Festive day. The Monday after Pentecost is usually a Bank Holiday in many European Countries. (For the Biblical narrative on the story of the Day of Pentecost refer to Acts of Apostles Chapter 2 Verse 1-38)

148) Answer: The Gentiles were people in the Bible outside of the ancient Jewish or Hebrew race. Jesus Christ interacted with numerous Gentiles during his ministry on earth. (Refer to Matthew Chapter 15 Verse 21-28; Matthew Chapter 8 Verse 5-13; John Chapter 4 Verse 1-26) Jesus Christ appeared to Saul (who later became Paul) to become his chosen vessel to preach the Gospel of Jesus Christ to Gentiles, Kings, and to the ancient people of Israel. (Refer to Acts of Apostles Chapter 9 Verse 15)

Ancient Jews had viewed ancient Gentiles as "uncommon and unclean." Apostle Peter had a stigma about Gentiles until he had a revelation vision from God (Refer to Acts of Apostles Chapter 10 Verse 9-22) in which God told him: "Do not call what I have cleansed uncommon or unclean." The Apostle Peter invited (on the instruction of God) the Gentile Cornelius and his family to his home in Joppa to be baptised in the Holy Ghost, which under ancient Jewish Customs back then would have made him (Peter) unclean.

Apostle Paul, during his ministry, had spoken out against this stigma and preached Jesus Christ to the ancient Gentile world (Refer to Romans Chapter 3 Verse 22; Romans Chapter 10 Verse 12; Galatians Chapter 3 Verse 28; Colossians Chapter 3 Verse 11)

Those that are in Christ Jesus (Gentiles, Jews, and all those that come to the knowledge of God) are cleansed from all their sins through the blood of Jesus Christ.

149) Answer: The ancient Ethiopian Eunuch was probably one of the most outstanding converts to Christianity in the Book of the Acts of Apostle. As the Biblical narrative puts it, an angel of God instructed Philip (one of the seven reputable officers chosen by the original twelve disciples that looked after the needy) to journey south along the road leading to Jerusalem where he encounters a man of Ethiopia, a Eunuch of great authority under Candace the Queen of Ethiopia who had charge of all her treasury came to Jerusalem to worship God and was returning back to his homeland. The Eunuch was sitting in his chariot reading a chapter from Prophet Isaiah when the Holy Spirit instructed Philip to go up to the Eunuch to find out whether he understood what he was reading. The Eunuch then asked Philip to come and sit with him in the Chariot to explain the place in the Scripture that he was reading: "He was led as a sheep to the slaughter; and as a lamb before its shearer is silent; so he opened not his mouth; in his humiliation, his justice was taken away, and who will declare his generation? For his life was taken from the earth." The Eunuch asked Philip who the Prophet Isaiah talking about. Philip then told Eunuch who Prophet Isaiah was writing about and told the Eunuch about Jesus Christ. The Eunuch believes on the spot that Jesus Christ is the Son of God and agrees to be baptised by Philip. (Refer to Acts of Apostles Chapter 8 Verse 26-39)

150) Answer: The gifts that the Wise Men from the East presented to Baby Jesus Christ were: Gold, Frankincense, and Myrrh (Refer to Matthew Chapter 2 Verse 10-12)

151) Answer: The New Testament Gospel of Luke states that Jesus Christ was about thirty years of age at the start of his Ministry.(Refer to Luke Chapter 3 Verse 23)

152) Answer: When Herod found out that he had been deceived by the Wise Men from the East, in a terrible rage he ordered the massacre of all male children in ancient Bethlehem and in all its surrounding districts from two years and under. (Refer to Matthew Chapter 2 Verse 16-18)

153) Answer: The Angel instructed Joseph in a dream to take Baby Jesus Christ and Mary and flee to ancient Egypt until the Angel confirmed it was safe to come back. Herod wanted to kill Baby Jesus Christ. Joseph, therefore, stayed in ancient Egypt with Baby Jesus Christ and Mary until the death of Herod. (Refer to Matthew Chapter 2 Verse 13-15)

154) Answer: According to the Biblical Narrative in the New Testament, the first miracle attributed to Jesus Christ was the turning of water into wine. (Refer to John Chapter 2 Verse 1-11)

Jesus Christ's miracle of turning water into wine at the Marriage of Cana draws symbolic reference to that similarly to Moses, in the Old Testament, turning the ancient Nile Egyptian River into blood. (Refer to Exodus Chapter 7 Verse 17) This would indicate an important symbolic link between Moses (through God's direction) as the first deliverer of the ancient Jews through their departure from ancient Egypt, and Jesus Christ as the Spiritual Saviour of the whole world. (Refer also to John Chapter 3 Verse 16-17)

155) Answer: "For God so loved the world that He gave us his only begotten son that whoever believes in Him should not perish but have everlasting life." (Refer to John Chapter 3 Verse 16)

156) Answer: "In the beginning was the Word and the Word was with God; and the Word was God." (Refer to John

Chapter 1 Verse 1) This is similar to the opening in the Book of Genesis. (Refer also to Genesis Chapter 1 Verse 1-2)

157) Answer: Ananias was the Disciple in the Book of Acts of Apostles (instructed by Jesus Christ in a vision) to "lay his hand" on Saul of Tarsus (who became Paul) so that he might receive his sight. (Refer to Acts Chapter 9 Verse 10-19)

158) Answer: Matthias was the apostle that replaced Judas Iscariot. Peter stood up and addressed about one hundred and twenty disciples in the Book of Acts of Apostles regarding the replacement of Judas Iscariot. Peter reminded them that scripture regarding Judas Iscariot had to be fulfilled when he betrayed Jesus Christ in the Garden of Gethsemane and foretold by King David when he wrote about it in the Book of Psalms. (Refer to Psalms 69 Verse 25)

Peter led the intercession with the other one hundred and twenty disciples to choose the right Apostle. After they had cast their lots, the lots fell on Matthias and he was the person that joined the eleven Apostles. (Refer to Acts of Apostles Chapter 1 Verse 20-26)

159) Answer: The Gospel of John in the New Testament showcases Jesus Christ in his goodness as the Son of God. John's Gospel differs from Matthew's Gospel in the sense that it is not chronological; it is topical. It revolves around "I am" statements of Jesus Christ, such as: "I am the Bread of life"; "I am the living bread which came down from heaven"; "I am the good shepherd"; "I am the resurrection and the life."(Refer to John Chapter 6 Verse 48; John Chapter 6 Verse 51; John Chapter 10 Verse 11; John Chapter 11 Verse 25)

John's Gospel is not only to reveal Jesus Christ in his deity or goodness but to ignite believing faith in his readers to reveal Jesus Christ as the Messiah and Son of God. The Gospel of

Luke carefully portrays Jesus Christ in his humanity as the Son of Man by tracing His (Jesus Christ) ancestry, birth, and early life.

Matthew's Gospel is the Gospel written by Matthew (who is a Jew) to the ancient Jews. Matthew writes painstakingly to his fellow countrymen and readers presenting Jesus Christ as The King of the Jews, and the long-anticipated Messiah. Through a carefully selected series of Old Testament quotations Matthew documents Jesus Christ's claim as the Christ, Messiah and the Saviour of the world. His (Jesus Christ's) genealogy, baptism, messages, and miracles all point to the implacable conclusion: Jesus Christ is Lord.

160) Answer: Jesus Christ cited a child as an example as being the greatest in the kingdom of heaven. (Refer to Matthew Chapter 18 Verse 1-5)

161) Answer: Jesus Christ was referring to Prophet Elijah in the Old Testament.

162) Answer: "Let not your heart be troubled; you believe in God, believe also in Me." (Refer to John Chapter 14 Verse 1)

163) Answer: The woman with the issue of blood was bleeding for twelve years. Under the ancient Jewish custom, she was considered an outcast. After seeing all the doctors in the land who could not heal her condition, she heard about Jesus Christ of Nazareth and had faith by saying: "If only I could touch the hem of his garment." Immediately, as she touched Jesus Christ's garment the bleeding ceased. (Refer to Mark Chapter 5 Verse 25-34)

164) Answer: They are called Canonical Gospels because they contain similar stories frequently in similar sequences. John's Gospel out of the four Gospel's is the only one that stands distinct. John's Gospel,is therefore not part of the three Canonical Gospels.

165) Answer: The reason why John's Gospel is not part of the Canonical or Synoptic Gospels is because it was written in a different style, tone, and manner.

166) Answer: In Luke Chapter 15 Verse 4-7, Jesus Christ tells a didactic story of the lost sheep when the Pharisees and Scribes complain about him (Jesus Christ) dinning with Sinners. The Parable of the Lost Sheep shares significant concepts such as loss, searching, and rejoicing. The Parable of the Lost Sheep shows God's response of going to great lengths to recover the Lost. The Rejoicing or Celebrating of the Lost Sheep with friends signifies God rejoicing with the Angels in heaven at the recovery of the Lost Sinners compared with the Religious Leaders which brought about the Parable. (Refer to Luke Chapter 15 Verse 4-7)

167) Answer: When Jesus Christ taught in the temple and preached the Gospel; the Scribes, Chief Priests, and Elders confronted him and asked by what authority He (Jesus Christ) was doing these things (Healing on the Sabbath Day, Receives, Eats with Sinners).

168) Answer: Peter and John, according to the narrative in the Book of Acts of Apostles. went up to the Temple of Beautiful at the ninth hour (mid-afternoon time) when they encountered a certain man who was lame from his mother's womb. The man was asking for charity donations from people as they entered the temple. As Peter and John were

about to enter the temple, the man saw them and was expecting to receive something from them when Peter asked the man to look at them. The man gave them his attention, hoping to receive something from Peter and John, when Peter replied: "Silver and Gold I do not have, but what I do have I give you; in the name of Jesus Christ of Nazareth, rise up and walk."

169) Answer: The Parable of the "Unjust Judge", "The Parable of the Persistent Widow", or "The Parable of the Importunate Widow" (all refer to the same Parable) was one of the Parables where he encouraged his disciples and listeners to always pray, be in faith, and not give up. The Parable was about a Judge who lacked compassion and is repeatedly approached by a necessitous widow seeking justice. At the outset, the Judge rejects the widow's demands but eventually upholds her requests so he will not be worn out by her persistence. (Refer to Luke Chapter 18 Verse 1-8)

170) Answer: Judas Iscariot betrayed Jesus Christ in the Garden of Gethsemane. He led the soldiers to where Jesus Christ was praying. Judas then kissed Jesus Christ to identify him to his captors. Judas Iscariot had all this figured out and well planned. According to Matthew's Gospel, Judas felt remorseful for what he had done. He returned the money and then committed suicide. (Refer to Matthew Chapter 27 Verse 3-5)

171) Answer: The Blind Beggar Bartimaeus shouted out: "Jesus Christ, Son of David, have mercy on me!" He was told to keep quiet by the multitude, but he cried out even louder. "Son of David, have mercy on me!" Jesus Christ stood still and commanded Bartimaeus to be brought to Him. (Refer to Mark Chapter 10 Verse 46-50)

172) Answer: This response was from Jesus Christ when a Pharisee came to test Him (Jesus Christ) in the Law of Moses in the Old Testament. Jesus Christ then replied and said: "'You shall love the Lord your God with all your heart, with all your soul, with all your mind, and with all your strength.' This is the first and great commandment. The second one is similar to the first one: 'You shall love your neighbour as yourself.' There is no other commandment greater than these." (Refer to Mark Chapter 12 Verse 28-34; Luke Chapter 10 Verse 25-37; Matthew Chapter 22 Verse 35-40)

173) Answer: The reason why Seven Deacons were chosen by the Apostles of the Early Church in the Book of Acts of Apostles was to enable the Apostles to concentrate on "Prayer and the Ministry of the Word" and to address a concern raised by Greek-speaking believers about their widows being overlooked in the daily Ministry. (Refer to Acts of Apostles Chapter 6 Verse 1-6) The twelve Apostles summoned the multitude of the disciples (which had grown) and said, "It is not desirable that we should leave or forsake the (Gospel) word of God and serve tables." (Refer to Acts of Apostles Chapter 6 Verse 2)

174) Answer: The Seven Deacons were:

- Stephen (who became the first Christian Martyr)
- Philip (The Evangelist)
- Prochorus
- Nicanor
- Timon
- Parmenas
- Nicholas

(Refer to Acts of Apostles Chapter 6 Verse 4-6)

175) Answer: The Six Pieces of the Armour of God mentioned in the Bible: (Refer to Ephesians Chapter 6 Verse 14-16)

- Belt of Truth
- Breast Plate of Righteousness
- Feet Fitted with the Gospel of Peace
- Shield of Faith
- Helmet of Salvation
- Sword of the Spirit (The Word of God)

176) Answer: Timothy was born in the Lycaonian City of Lystra (Asia Minor). His mother was a Jew who had become a Christian Believer and his father a Greek. Apostle Paul had met him on his Second Missionary Journey of Asia Minor and became a companion of Paul and Silas.

177) Answer: It was Apostle Paul's desire to encourage and mentor the young Evangelist and Apostle Timothy in the Gospel Christian Ministry. Apostle Paul gave Timothy much counsel as counsel is useful for Christians today as it was for Timothy. He (Apostle Paul) urged Timothy to be watchful and to challenge false doctrines and greedy motives but to instead pursue righteousness, godliness, faith, love, perseverance, and gentleness that befits a person called by God. Apostle Paul also warned Timothy that his (Timothy's) teaching would come under attack as people will desert the truth for ear-itching words. (Refer to 2 Timothy Chapter 4 Verse 3-5) (Refer to I Timothy Chapter 1-Chapter 6, II Timothy Chapter 1-Chapter 4)

178) Answer: Lydia was a hospitable and generous character mentioned in the Book of Acts of Apostles who offered Apostle Paul and his companion hospitality and

accommodation on their Christian Missionary journey. She was a Macedonian Greek. She was a trader of velvet material from the City of Ancient Thyatria in Greece (Asia Minor). Lydia heard the Gospel of Jesus Christ preached by Apostle Paul when he was preaching in Macedonia. She and her household were baptised after hearing the Gospel of Jesus Christ.

179) Answer: Several ancient Jewish believers who had moved away from Judaism into Christianity wanted to change the course of their lives to avoid persecution by their fellow Jewish counterparts. The writer of the Book of Hebrews is unknown but can be perceived to be an Ancient Jewish Christian. The writer's appeal is drawn on the basis of the superiority of Christ over the Judaic system. Jesus Christ is better than Angels, for they worship him. He is better than Moses for He created him. He is better than the Aaronic Priesthood, for His (Jesus Christ) sacrifice was once for all time. He is better than the law, for He (Jesus Christ) reflects a better covenant. In other words, there is more to be gained in Christ than to be lost in Judaism. Forging on in Christ creates self-discipline, patience, long-suffering, and faith.

180) Answer: The fruit of the Holy Spirit can be defined as when an individual or a group of Christian believers that abide by or are living in accordance with the Holy Spirit mentioned in the Book or Epistle of Galatians Chapter 5 Verse 22-23. The fruit of the Holy Spirit is:

- Love
- Joy
- Peace
- Longsuffering
- Kindness
- Goodness

- Faithfulness
- Gentleness
- Self-control

181) Answer: True

182) Answer: True

183) Answer: False

184) Answer: True

185) Answer: True

186) Answer: False

187) Answer: True

188) Answer: False

189) Answer: False

190) Answer: True

191) Answer: False

192) Answer: True

193) Answer: False

194) Answer: True

195) Answer: True

196) Answer: True

197) Answer: True

198) Answer: True

199) Answer: False

200) Answer: True

201) Answer: False

202) Answer: D

203) Answer: A

204) Answer: E

205) Answer: D

206) Answer: A

207) Answer: E

208) Answer: C

209) Answer: B

210) Answer: C

211) Answer: A

212) Answer: C

213) Answer: E

214) Answer: D

215) Answer: C

216) Answer: E

217) Answer: D

218) Answer: C

219) Answer: E

220) Answer: D

221) Answer: A

222) Answer: C

223) Answer: B

224) Answer: D

225) Answer: A

226) Answer: C

227) Answer: E

228) Answer: A

229) Answer: B

230) Answer: C

231) Answer: A

232) Answer: E

233) Answer: B

234) Answer: B

235) Answer: D

236) Answer: A

237) Answer: E

238) Answer: B

239) Answer: A

240) Answer: C

241) Answer: E

242) Answer: B

243) Answer: C

244) Answer: C

245) Answer: A

246) Answer: D

247) Answer: E

248) Answer: B

249) Answer: A

250) Answer: C

251) Answer: A

252) Answer: B

253) Answer: E

254) Answer: C

255) Answer: A

256) Answer: E

257) Answer: A

258) Answer: D

259) Answer: D

260) Answer: A

261) Answer: C

262) Answer: C

263) Answer: A

264) Answer: C

265) Answer: E

266) Answer: B

267) Answer: B

268) Answer: E

269) Answer: D

270) Answer: E

271) Answer: A

272) Answer: E

273) Answer: E

274) Answer: D

275) Answer: A

276) Answer: B

277) Answer: E

278) Answer: B

279) Answer: C

280) Answer: True

281) Answer: True
282) Answer: True
283) Answer: False
284) Answer: False
285) Answer: False
286) Answer: True
287) Answer: True
288) Answer: False
289) Answer: True
290) Answer: B – True
291) Answer: True
292) Answer: True
293) Answer: True
294) Answer: True
295) Answer: True
296) Answer: A
297) Answer: A
298) Answer: C
299) Answer: E
300) Answer: A
301) Answer: E
302) Answer: C
303) Answer: B
304) Answer: E
305) Answer: D
306) Answer: E
307) Answer: B

308) Answer: A
309) Answer: E
310) Answer: B
311) Answer: B
312) Answer: C
313) Answer: D
314) Answer: B
315) Answer: A
316) Answer: E
317) Answer: E
318) Answer: D
319) Answer: C
320) Answer: A
321) Answer: C
322) Answer: E
323) Answer: A
324) Answer: D
325) Answer: D
326) Answer: A
327) Answer: E
328) Answer: E
329) Answer: B
330) Answer: D
331) Answer: A
332) Answer: C
333) Answer: E
334) Answer: B

335) Answer: D	362) Answer: C
336) Answer: E	363) Answer: B
337) Answer: E	364) Answer: B
338) Answer: D	365) Answer: E
339) Answer: A	366) Answer: A
340) Answer: C	367) Answer: C
341) Answer: E	368) Answer: E
342) Answer: B	369) Answer: B
343) Answer: C	370) Answer: A
344) Answer: D	371) Answer: C
345) Answer: C	372) Answer: B
346) Answer: C	373) Answer: D
347) Answer: A	374) Answer: A
348) Answer: E	375) Answer: D
349) Answer: B	376) Answer: C
350) Answer: A	377) Answer: E
351) Answer: C	378) Answer: A
352) Answer: B	379) Answer: E
353) Answer: A	380) Answer: C
354) Answer: C	381) Answer: E
355) Answer: D	382) Answer: D
356) Answer: C	383) Answer: E
357) Answer: E	384) Answer: B
358) Answer: B	385) Answer: E
359) Answer: C	386) Answer: True
360) Answer: C	387) Answer: False
361) Answer: E	388) Answer: False

389) Answer: True

390) Answer: True

391) Answer: True

392) Answer: True

393) Answer: False

394) Answer: True

395) Answer: True

396) Answer False

397) Answer: True

398) Answer: False

399) Answer: True

400) Answer: True

401) Answer: A

402) Answer: D

403) Answer: C

404) Answer: E

405) Answer: C

406) Answer: C

407) Answer: A

408) Answer: B

409) Answer: D

410) Answer: B

411) Answer: A

412) Answer: A

413) Answer: C

414) Answer: B

415) Answer: D

416) Answer: B

417) Answer: E

418) Answer: E

419) Answer: A

420) Answer: D

421) Answer: B

422) Answer: C

423) Answer: E

424) Answer: D

425) Answer: A

BIBLIOGRAPHY

❖ *The Holy Bible, New King James Version* (1982) by Thomas Nelson
❖ *The Holy Bible, New Living Translation* (1996) by Tyndale House
❖ *An Encyclopedia of Bible Facts* (1988) by Mark Water
❖ *Encylopedia of Britannica Military Leaders*
❖ Jewish Virtual Library
❖ *History Zeva'it shel Erez Yisrael* (1964)
❖ *Antiquities of the Jews Book VII*, Chapter 1 by Flavius Josephus
❖ *The Message Bible*, by Eugene H. Peterson
❖ *Kings of the Bible*, by Jean-Pierre Isbouts
❖ *Topics in West African History* by A. Adu Boahen and J.F. Ade Ajayi

Printed in Great Britain
by Amazon

19987279R00102